UNDER PRESSURE

DENIS SARTAIN & MARIA KATSAROU

UNDER PRESSURE

UNDERSTANDING AND MANAGING
THE PRESSURE AND STRESS OF WORK

First published in 2011 by Marshall Cavendish Business
An imprint of Marshall Cavendish International

PO Box 65829
London EC1P 1NY
United Kingdom
info@marshallcavendish.co.uk

and

1 New Industrial Road
Singapore 536196
genrefsales@sg.marshallcavendish.com
www.marshallcavendish.com/genref

Other Marshall Cavendish offices:
Marshall Cavendish International (Asia) Private Limited, 1 New Industrial Road, Singapore 536196 • Marshall Cavendish Corporation, 99 White Plains Road, Tarrytown NY 10591–9001, USA • Marshall Cavendish International (Thailand) Co Ltd, 253 Asoke, 12th Floor, Sukhumvit 21 Road, Klongtoey Nua, Wattana, Bangkok 10110, Thailand • Marshall Cavendish (Malaysia) Sdn Bhd, Times Subang, Lot 46, Subang Hi-Tech Industrial Park, Batu Tiga, 40000 Shah Alam, Selangor Darul Ehsan, Malaysia

A CIP record for this book is available from the British Library

ISBN 978-981-4302-63-0

Cover design by OpalWorks
Printed and bound in the United Kingdom by CPI William Clowes

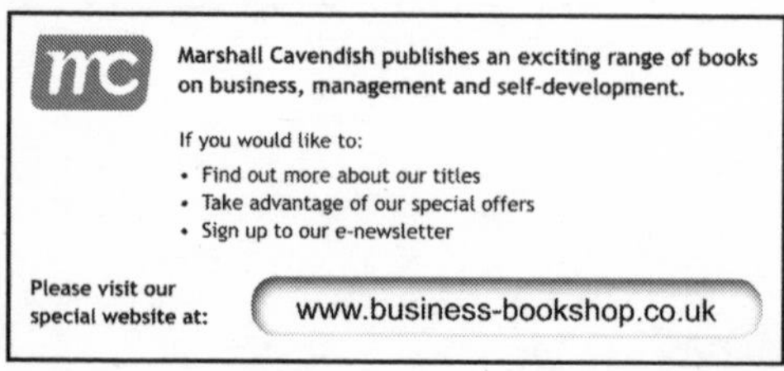

To my children Louis and Kiera, who will enter the workplace armed with the ability to keep things in perspective, be responsible and work hard, and help sustain others around them.

—Denis

To Alex my brother, Petros my father, and my mother Lucia.

—Maria

CONTENTS

PART II: MANAGING PRESSURE & STRESS

INTRODUCTION

In our job we see a lot of stressed people. Whether in seminars, courses, clinic settings, or through HR, we have met many bright, ambitious, hardworking people, from all over the world, who reveal to us the pressures and stress they face in the workplace. The pressures stem from many sources—self-perception, problems with bosses or colleagues, guilt arising from making people redundant—and are not confined to the self, but extend to the communities these people operate in.

Over the past ten years, war, natural disasters, and economic fallouts have become more frequent. The year 2009 saw the severest winter in 30 years in the UK; massive snow storms in the United States, resulting in a significant number of deaths; floods in the Philippines; mudslides in Brazil; and huge fires in Greece, Australia and California. In 2010, we have already witnessed the earthquake in Haiti and the devastating floods in Pakistan. The financial crisis produced severe unemployment and hardship for many and seems set to continue to do so as governments worldwide introduce austerity packages to reduce their deficits.

These events affect our mood and sense of "reality." While we may not be directly or immediately affected by them, we know that we may well be eventually. We know that there are some things we can do to help—humanitarian aid, environmental protection, etc.—and at the same time we also realize that there are things which are beyond our control.

So too with our personal and professional lives. There are things we can affect, and things we can't. However, we aren't able to think about these things in as orderly a manner—because it's personal.

As we go about our daily lives, we have good days and bad days; sometimes we are more successful at dealing with the bad days than others, and some people appear to be better at dealing with pressure than others, while some people simply aren't able to cope with pressure at all. The consequences can be devastating.

The people on our pressure-management programmes work incredibly hard in their jobs and are very loyal employees. They attend our programmes to find out how they can manage pressure while trying to maintain their own high standards of work, be more effective with their team mates, and continue to be high contributors to their company's success. Such conscientiousness comes at a price: Those most likely to suffer stress-related illness and complaints are a company's biggest asset—their most conscientious people.

How is this so? Conscientiousness can be defined as the trait of being painstaking and careful. If the following concepts describe you quite accurately then you are probably highly conscientious: self-disciplined; taking care in what you do; thorough; highly organized; tending to think carefully before acting; motivated by achievement; hardworking; reliable.

Thinking about these, rate yourself on a scale of 1 to 10 (1=Low, 10=High) for conscientiousness. People who rate themselves below 5, i.e., those on the less conscientious end of the scale, are less likely to suffer from stress. On all our pressure-management programmes, whether voluntary or prescribed, we hardly ever encounter anyone who rates himself below 6.

So an organization's most conscientious employees are the most likely to suffer from the negative effects of pressure. Luckily the ones we meet are also conscientious enough to take the initiative to manage that stress—and you too, by choosing this book, have also taken that step.

This book is about learning to live and work under pressure; or more specifically, it is about managing the *negative* aspects of pressure, because not all pressure is negative. Some pressures can be extremely pleasurable and rewarding—marriage, relocation, outstanding achievements—and without any form of pressure we might never achieve anything. But even positive pressure, when there is too much of it, can have harmful consequences to the unknowing.

In this book we take the view that individuals—once they understand their own relationship to and capacity for handling pressure—must themselves assume responsibility for managing the challenge it presents, and have the courage to seek advice or guidance if they need to. We believe at the same time that leaders in all organizations must take responsibility for recognizing when someone is feeling overwhelmed to the point of exhaustion or paralysis, and to understand that this is only a response, and not a failing or weakness. We need to encourage a culture that views managing pressure as being as important as servicing a car—vital to keep it operating smoothly and reliably.

Looking after yourself is the key to managing pressure, and in the following pages, we hope to present you with ideas, facts and information that will make it easier for you to do so.

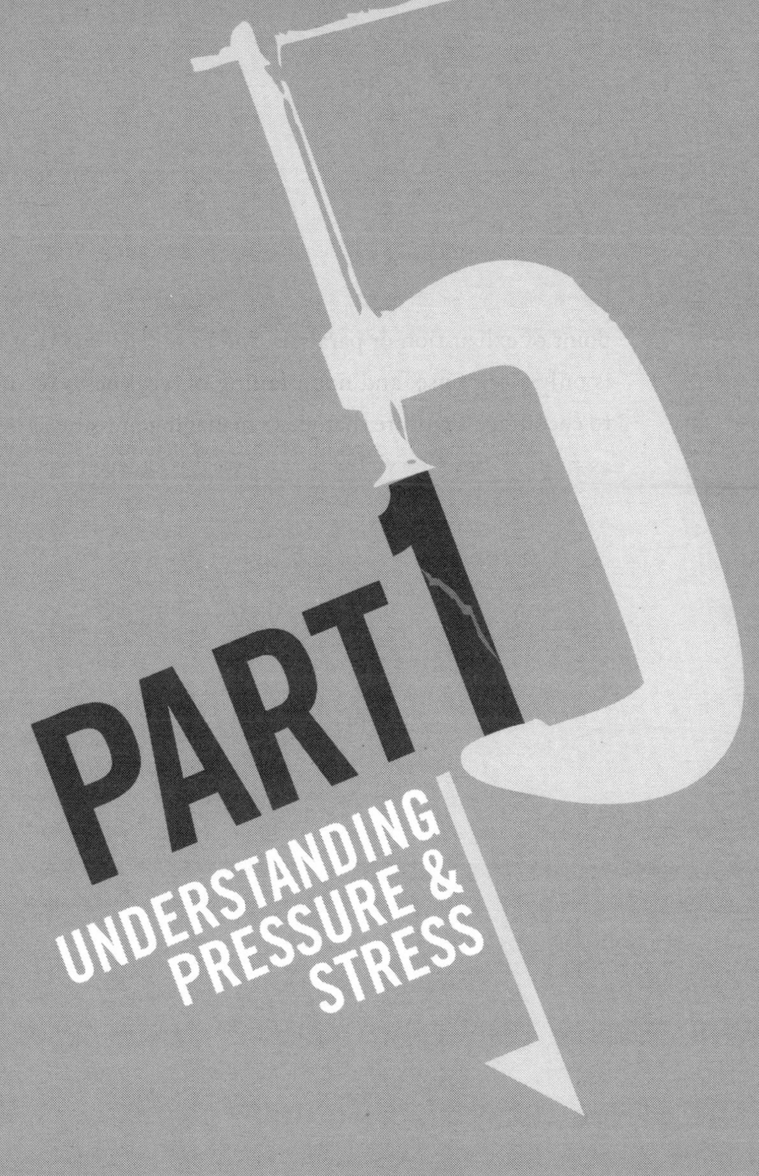

PART 1
UNDERSTANDING PRESSURE & STRESS

WHAT'S HAPPENING IN THE WORLD OF WORK?

Why there is so much pressure to deal with, why now, and how pressure escalates

In 2009, over a period of 24 months, 24 employees of France Telecom committed suicide, many of them blaming work as the reason they wanted to end their lives. On 9 September 2009, a technician in Troyes, southeast of Paris, stabbed himself in front of other staff after being told his job was to be cut. In August another employee, a 53-year-old father of three, killed himself in Brittany. "Infantile" management and "difficulties around his rank within the company" were blamed as reasons for his death. The same month, a 28-year-old worker was found dead in his garage in a town in the east of France, having left a note that not only talked of his girlfriend but mentioned how "helpless" and "angry" he felt over issues at work. In Marseille a 52-year-old employee killed himself on 14 July 2009, leaving a note in which he blamed "overwork" and "management by terror." He wrote, "I am committing suicide because of my work at France Telecom. That's the only reason." Other cases followed.[1]

It's rarely possible to blame suicide on a single factor—it's usually a combination of factors—but in this case, people attributed their despair *mainly* to work.

Information: A double-edged sword

Why does work become overwhelming for some? And why is it apparently more stressful now than ever before?

The world of work operates within the larger context of the world as we know it and there's a *lot* happening out there. Once, people depended on the 9-o'clock news and the daily paper to keep themselves informed. In the workplace, companies could bring in consultants to explain the work environment; managers could make claims about company direction and policy safe in the knowledge that the information they disseminated would only be challenged by relatively few well-informed, well-read people. Whether this was a wholly positive thing or not, it meant that people were generally a lot easier to manage. They depended on what people told them, often only trusting in one or two sources.

Now, we have instant access to myriad sources of information: blogs, academic opinions, uninformed opinions, lay opinions, unqualified opinions, celebrity opinions, outright propaganda, spin, reported events from conventional sources, news channels from within the country and without—all accessible at the same time.

Executives making announcements may now find that their sources are being checked by their audiences there and then. Chief executives talking about company profitability and prospects face an audience of employees, shareholders and media who can verify the data through their mobile phones—possibly while they listen to the presentation. Consultants and advisors have their advice second-guessed and scrutinized via the internet. Leaders in all contexts, and those they lead, are challenged to stay up to date, and to make judgments—almost continually—about the authenticity, veracity, desirability and completeness of what they present or read.

This is one of the most significant changes in the world of work in the last decade. While in many ways it is a good thing—the democratization of information putting power into the hands of the many, rather than the few—it also puts tremendous pressures on both leaders and their teams.

Cognitive dissonance

When you hear someone say one thing and watch them do something else, you experience what is known as "cognitive dissonance." When *you* say one thing and then do another, you also experience cognitive dissonance. Cognitive dissonance, then, is the feeling you get when you sense a gap between what is *given* and what is *known*.

The increase in availability of information, as outlined above, has led to the increase in instances of cognitive dissonance—the more you know, the greater the chances that the stories don't add up.

In today's corporate world, it is one of the major causes of pressure. Cognitive dissonance is, to begin with, an unpleasant state of heightened arousal.[2] This means that stress levels increase considerably in response to dissonance, resulting in negative behaviour, physical ailments, feelings of hopelessness, or even self-harm. What's more, when faced with dissonance, we are motivated to reduce the discrepancy. This may mean we stop pretending that everything is alright and stop working so hard; equally it could mean we keep working, coping with worry as best we can, and resenting those who place us in this situation. Both these responses to the originating dissonance are stressful.[3]

In one of the earliest and best-known studies on cognitive dissonance, one group of subjects was paid $1 for telling someone who'd just completed a boring task that it was very interesting. A second group was paid $20 for the same task. Both groups were being made to engage in what is called "attitude-discrepant behaviour," that is, behaviour that ran counter to their actual thoughts and feelings. Both groups were then asked to rate their liking for the task. Interestingly, the group paid less rated the task as significantly more interesting than the group paid 20 times more. Why would that be? Leon Festinger, who conducted the study, hypothesized that it is much easier to tell a lie for a large amount of money than a small one. But in order to feel better about it, those who were paid only $1 *made themselves believe that what they were doing was very interesting.*

This aspect of rationalizing our beliefs to fit our behaviour pervades so many aspects of our working lives. We are more likely to change our beliefs about something or someone than to change the way we act.

We are led to believe that working hard will lead to achievement and reward. We also believe that providing for our families is important and that they need us to be around them, to spend time with them, to grow up happy, healthy and balanced. So what happens to the executive who works extremely long hours to achieve the company's goals, gets paid well, yet does not see his children except on the weekends? How does he deal with conflicting beliefs?

The holding of two conflicting beliefs simultaneously is very common. So too are our efforts to deal with them. Smokers commonly hold two conflicting beliefs: (1) Smoking is bad for me and I can die from it; and (2) smoking calms me down and things are bad at the moment so I need it. In order to lessen the dissonance, smokers, rather than not smoking, will rationalize why they need to smoke, how they only smoke a little, or how much worse their health would be if they stopped and had to deal with pressure without a coping mechanism and so on. People who drink use the same rationalizing process to lessen dissonance, just as most people do in any number of settings.

Lessening dissonance by altering or manipulating our beliefs does not necessarily change the facts. Changing our behaviour is the way to effectively stop lying, smoking, drinking, or working the kind of hours that destroy our health and our families.

In order to manage cognitive dissonance, we rely on certain basic principles:

- The more we can be ourselves, the happier we are.
- The more we feel others are being themselves with us, the more comfortable we feel.
- The more we feel that facts presented to us are truthfully presented, the more willing we are to accept them.

- Even unpleasant facts and realities can be made more palatable if we do not have to deal with cognitive dissonance.

What's common to these principles is our need to be "authentic." In a world of spin and manipulation, we have become cynical of the promises made to us, and the sales pitches we in turn have to deliver. Leaders must ask themselves, "Why should anyone be led by me? What can people depend on me for?"[4]

The increase in cognitive dissonance in the workplace isn't deliberate but is partly the result of a management style still trying to catch up with some of the realities and practicalities of the technological age as we have discussed earlier. It is also caused by the pace of change.

Change and stress

Change is a corporate reality. Most people know it is inevitable, but still find it difficult to handle the way in which it is managed.

Mergers and acquisitions, cost reductions and other changes are on the increase, as emerging markets in countries like China, Brazil and India take advantage of companies and countries in the West and Japan stumbling under debt. In business today, it's not uncommon to see extraordinarily successful companies with active acquisition strategies finding themselves becoming the acquired—the hunter becoming the hunted.

In these situations uncertainty and fear about the future exist at all levels. When people don't know what's going to happen to them, they feel under pressure. Senior executives can be most at risk in a merger as the dominant company puts in people they can "trust" even if the company they have acquired is operating brilliantly with its incumbent team.

A study published in the July/August 2008 issue of the *Journal of Business Strategy* suggests that mergers and acquisitions destroy leadership continuity in target companies' top management teams for at least a decade following a deal. The study found that target companies lose 21 per cent of their executives each year for at least ten years following an acquisition—more than double the turnover experienced in non-merged firms.

This is another example of cognitive dissonance. People who are involved in mergers and acquisitions are told that what is happening to them is for the good of the company and will help it to survive; yet it is also clear to them that it could result in the loss of their job and income. Having to act as if it's all fine produces feelings of stress and anxiety for everyone.

In 1996 we were asked to consult by the board of a large British shipping company who had been acquired by a competitor in the US. Our job was to prepare the board for the takeover and to advise on possible scenarios the management team might experience. These ranged from the possibility that the new owners might appoint a new managing director, that they might keep the team intact, or that people might be asked for their car keys and escorted from the building on the day of the takeover. At least the people at the top were being prepared for alternative future conditions—those below needed to depend on the authenticity of messages coming from that team.

Our experience with executives and people in the workplace at all levels is that the more awareness they have, the more control they feel they have over their options, and the more time they have to seek help and advice.

Control over our lives requires us to have information about our present situation; this information allows us to properly consider our options. Hence when this information is dubious, or even outright false, it puts our futures and the futures of those who depend on us in the balance. We suffer stress as a result.

Honest information, therefore, is the key. People are owed that honesty, however unpalatable, so they can make decisions and feel they have some control. When people don't have the information or answers—or inadequate or inaccurate information—they often seek to address the cognitive dissonance they feel by making it up, sometimes with harmful consequences to themselves and the organization.

THE PSYCHOLOGY AND PHYSIOLOGY OF STRESS

The process of becoming stressed, the symptoms of stress, and the price we pay for neglecting its presence in our lives

Who gets stressed? The answer is doctors, psychologists, health workers, refuse collectors, factory workers, teachers, engineers, fitness instructors, executives, managers, employees—in fact, everyone and anyone. It is an inevitable aspect of the human condition. It is the *way* that we deal with stress that makes the difference.

The impact of stress in the workplace

The workplace best demonstrates the scale of the issue in the Western world, as well as the importance of having ways to stay mentally healthy.

In the UK, occupational stress is a massive problem. It is now the most commonly reported reason for people taking sick leave.

- In the year 2007/08, 13.5 million working days were lost to work-related stress, at a cost to society of £3.5 billion.
- In 2002, 250,000 people considered that they were made ill (anxiety or depression) by their work.
- Based on statistics for 2002, some 7,000 people suffered severe nervous breakdowns caused by their work; a conclusion was drawn from these statistics that between 7,000 and 250,000 people per annum suffer from severe psychiatric injury caused at work alone. (Health and Safety Executive—HSE)
- The direct cost of absence due to stress for companies with more than 100,000 employees is annually estimated to be US$10–12 million for the retail sector, and US$18–25 million for the transportation and communications sector. (Henderson Global Investors 2005 Survey[5])

Statistics for other countries are equally revealing. In Canada, for example:

- The cost of work time lost to stress is C$12 billion per year;
- From 1992 to 1998, the proportion of Canadian women who felt "severe stress" rose by 23%, while for men it climbed 25%;
- Stress as a reason for absence has increased 316% since 1995;
- A 2003 survey on work–life conflict, which surveyed more than 31,000 workers, found that more than 50% felt stressed, 33% felt burned-out

or depressed, 25% thought of quitting their jobs at least once a week or more, and 10% reported high absenteeism due to emotional, physical or mental fatigue.

- The direct cost of absenteeism totals C$4.5 billion each year. (Canadian Centre of Occupational Health and Safety)
- Employees under sustained stress are likely to suffer:
  - 3 times more heart problems, back problems;
  - 5 times more of certain cancers;
  - 2–3 times more conflicts, mental-health problems, infections, injuries; and
  - 2 times more substance abuse.
- Mental health claims are the fastest growing category of disability costs in Canada. (Manulife Financial Group)
- Emotional distress and mental illness account for 20–30% of all employee absenteeism and industrial accidents, and mental/emotional problems at work exceeded physical causes as the primary reason for worker absenteeism for the first time ever in 1998. (Canadian Mental Health Association)

There is a similar story in the USA:

- Job stress is estimated to cost American industry $300 billion a year, more than the net profits of all the Fortune 500 companies combined and ten times the costs of all strikes;
- 40% of job turnover is due to job stress;
- 60–80% of on-the-job accidents are stress-related;

- 75–90% of all visits to primary care physicians are for stress-related complaints or conditions;
- Health care expenditures are nearly 50% greater for workers who report high stress levels. (American Institute of Stress)
- More than half of the 550 million working days lost each year because of absenteeism are due to stress. (European Agency for Safety & Health at Work)

Claiming for stress

Employees have generally found that making claims against their employers for work-related stress is not easy. This is chiefly because since people find different things stressful, stress in the workplace is difficult to define. In the UK, recent court rulings—such as *Walker* v. *Northumberland Council* and *Barber* v. *Somerset County Council*—led to the Court of Appeal laying down a set of guidelines that makes it very difficult for people to establish claims against employers. In arriving at the rulings and in laying down the guidelines, the Court of Appeal sought to apply the principles of fairness that apply to all judgements and, in doing so, made it clear how difficult it is to prove stress.

The bottom-line for everyone in the workplace is to learn to look after yourself. This focus on individual responsibility means not allowing yourself to become debilitated and then seeking to apportion blame for what has happened to you. Most people don't start looking after their stress levels until they have been *forced to* by ill-health. Learning to recognize stress and its symptoms is the first step to effective self-management.

What is stress?

A lot of people use the word "stress" to describe pressure.

We expect that everyone ought to be able to take some pressure. In the current corporate environment, it's imperative. Everyone must be able to operate under a certain amount of pressure. In fact, we believe that pressure can be and is generally positive—but stress is not. Stress is the stage we get to when we have gone beyond our pressure threshold. But how do we know when someone has moved from an acceptable level of pressure to stress?

When we are stressed beyond our pressure threshold, we start to make mistakes, make poor judgments, have poorer interactions and generally have a reduced quality of life.

Stress is cumulative. When we exceed our threshold and stay within the danger zone for too long, even taking some time off may not necessarily bring us back to our optimum performance level. The longer we stay stressed, the more it begins to affect our daily lives; our health begins to suffer. The longer we go on without addressing it, the worse it becomes, and we start to suffer physical illness. And if we persist in ignoring our stress levels, we run the ultimate risk of breakdown—the extreme end of the stress spectrum.

When this happens, people have to take time off from work—sometimes days, weeks, months and occasionally years. Breakdown or other illness caused by stress is the body's way of forcing us to take a break.

Can stress be good?

The following graph shows the relationship between one's performance and demands—that may include anything from

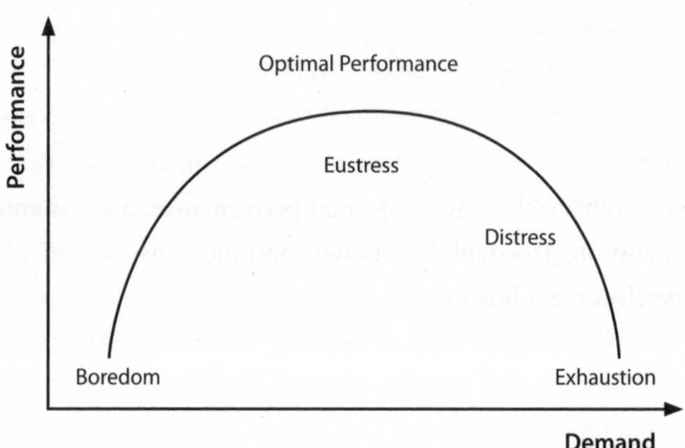

workload to pressure from other people and financial pressure.[6]

For each individual, there is a point of optimal performance, or "eustress," at which he is stretched to a level where the outcome of pressure is still positive. Before reaching this point, the individual would be experiencing boredom, if for example he was engaged in repetitive work or an undemanding job for a long period of time and hence finding no stimulation or interest anymore. If demands or pressure were to continue to increase beyond the individual's optimal performance point, then he or she would start being unable to cope, and go into the "distress" phase and eventually "exhaustion." The effects of pressure are now negative and performance suffers as well. This also explains why quite often people even though they try really hard feel their output is actually decreasing the more effort they put in.

Everybody needs a certain amount of pressure in order to "perform" and this varies in degree—meaning that some people seem to be able to take on more pressure while others tolerate much less.

This graph can serve as a reminder that all individuals operate on their own stress continuum, and have their own points of boredom, optimal performance, distress and exhaustion. To establish our own continuum, we need to ask ourselves the following:

- What are our personal "signals" for each phase?
- How do we experience boredom? What are the symptoms?
- How do we know when we are at our personal point of optimal performance?
- How do we know that we are entering the distress or even exhaustion phase? What are our strategies to prevent that?

The relativity of stress

As we reflected before, defining stress is difficult because our thresholds for pressure are so varied. What causes one person stress may not cause it for another. People in organizations have different responses to different situations. For example, how people react to news of, say, downsizing varies greatly. Some people will worry from the moment they hear about it till the process is complete, while others may not worry initially but become more concerned as time goes by. Some people take their excessively busy days at work home with them, while others are able to leave the job at work—the same people can still be highly effective and motivated. The way in which we process information has a great bearing on how we individually react to pressure and experience stress.

Could there be no such thing as stress then?—simply circumstances to which we have reactions both positive and negative? When dealing with our reaction, we need to recognize that any emotion whether positive or negative can become problematic without the right balance. Love can become smothering, anger can become murderous, caring can become claustrophobic, conscientiousness can become obsessive, and so on.

Applying some control over our thoughts, feelings, and emotions is what most people do successfully most of the time; but when we are out of balance we become stressed.

> Anyone can be angry, that is easy, but to be angry with the right person to the right degree, at the right time, for the right purpose, in the right way, that is not easy.
>
> —Aristotle, *The Nicomachean Ethics*

Defining stress

As stress depends so much on the individual's perceptions, a definition of stress must cover most people most of the time; it is necessary therefore for us to generalize. There are as many attempts to define stress as there are books about it. The Health and Safety Executive in the UK (HSE) describes it as

> The adverse reaction people have to excessive pressure or other types of demands people place on them.

This definition relates to the workplace, where the HSE has tried to break down the hazards and potential stressors in an organization and in so doing identify areas of stress. But this doesn't actually describe what stress is. Nor do any of the following definitions which describe the effects rather than the essence of stress:

> Stress is the unwanted outcome of too much pressure.[7]

> In psychology, stress is a physical or psychological stimulus which when impinging upon an individual produces strain or disequilibrium.[8]

> Stress is a word derived from the Latin word *stringere*, meaning to draw tight.... External forces (load) are seen as exerting pressure upon an individual, producing strain.[9]

We prefer to define stress as a *process*. It is the process by which we allow external events and demands, as well as our own internal demands, fears, beliefs, to reach varying degrees of discomfort and ultimately, if not addressed, sickness. *So, stress is an internal response to externally and internally generated stimuli.*

The physiological basis of stress

The process by which we get stressed is the same primeval process we use to help us survive. In prehistoric times, our survival depended on our ability to answer a very simple question when presented with a situation: "Is this safe for me or not?" A negative answer to this question would trigger the production of adrenalin. This is also commonly known as the "fight or flight" response.

This term, coined by the American physiologist Walter Cannon, is commonly used to describe the way in which the body reacts to stress. Cannon originally studied this response in animals, but it was later found to also be present in humans. When our ancestors came across a threat—sometimes large and with teeth—they needed to decide very quickly if they should fight or run away. At the first stage of the fight-or-flight response, the sympathetic nervous system is activated. This causes the whole body to respond. Adrenaline and nor-adrenaline are released, making the person more alert. Blood is re-routed from the internal organs and the skin to muscles that create movement. The heart-rate, the power of heart contractions, and rate of breathing are increased. The body begins to convert stored glycogen into glucose. All of these changes give the body a large amount of energy over a short period of time so that the individual may either fight effectively, or run away.

This process, and the response it produces, is still in us today, but isn't really necessary within the corporate environment. We hardly need the additional strength and speed that adrenaline will give us to enable us to leap across the board-room table and grapple with a perceived threat, nor do we use that additional energy to make a bolt for the door and leg it down the corridor. And yet our body undergoes the same chemical changes when presented with stressful situations.

To compound this, sometimes our responses to stress can be irrational and excessive. Daniel Goleman, the author of *Emotional Intelligence*, refers to this phenomenon as "emotional hijacking," in which the amygdalae (the part of our brains responsible for emotional matters) seize control over what we do before the neocortex (the thinking brain) can come to a rational decision.[10]

Stress *is* real—it can be seen and felt

So stress has a very real psychological and physiological effect. There have been various studies into the links between stress and illness, perhaps one of the best-known being the Social Readjustment Rating Scale (SRRS). In 1967, the psychiatrists Thomas Holmes and Richard Rahe examined 5,000 patient records and made a list of 43 life events of varying seriousness which had occurred in the months preceding the onset of the patient's illness.[11] Each of the events was assigned a value from zero to one hundred. The life events included in the list were not necessarily negative events; some in fact were happy events such as getting married and Christmas. The underlying assumption of the test was that stress is created by change and how much control we have or perceive we have over this change.

You can examine this chart for yourself. Add up your score for relevant events over the last 24 months.

Rank	Life event	Mean Value
1	Death of a spouse	100
2	Divorce	73
3	Marital separation	65
4	Jail term	63
5	Death of close family member	63
6	Personal injury or illness	63
7	Marriage	50
8	Fired at work	47
9	Marital reconciliation	45
10	Retirement	45

No.	Life Event	Score
11	Change in health of family member	44
12	Pregnancy	40
13	Sex difficulties	39
14	Gain of new family member	39
15	Business readjustment	39
16	Change in financial state	38
17	Death of a close friend	37
18	Change in different line of work	36
19	Change in number of arguments with spouse	35
20	Mortgage over $10,000	31
21	Foreclosure of mortgage or loan	30
22	Change in responsibilities at work	29
23	Son or daughter leaving home	29
24	Trouble with in-laws	29
25	Outstanding achievement	28
26	Spouse begins or stops work	26
27	Begin or end school	26
28	Change in living conditions	25
29	Revision of personal habits	24
30	Trouble with boss	23
31	Change in work hours or conditions	20
32	Change in residence	20
33	Change in schools	20
34	Change in recreation	19
35	Change in church activities	19
36	Change in social activities	18
37	Mortgage or loan less than $10,000	17
38	Change in sleeping habits	16
39	Change in number of family get-togethers	15
40	Change in eating habits	15
41	Vacation	13
42	Christmas	12
43	Minor violations of the law.	11
	TOTAL	___

0–149 Average chance of developing stress-related illness.

150–299 Moderate risk of developing stress-related illness.

≥300 Higher-than-average risk of developing stress-related illness in future

Studies have shown that people who experience significant life changes (scores of 300 and over) are more susceptible to physical and mental illness than those with lower ratings. In particular, it was those changes deemed "uncontrollable" by participants that correlated with the onset of illness.

The more control we have over our lives, the more comfortable we tend to feel. When we are unable to control what happens to us, we can positively take steps to reduce our stress levels by understanding why we are not in control.

The field of stress is complex and full of contradictions. Medical practitioners deal with people suffering from stress-related illnesses on a daily basis. Doctors increasingly have to deal with the physiological aspects of stress, knowing that the patient could benefit from some psychological help which might require a few more minutes of TLC and chat, but they are often hamstrung by the fact that there's a waiting room full of patients, and an extra five minutes means passing it all the way down the line. The patient is then given a pharmacological approach to stress management. While these practitioners are faced with everyday evidence of what some people predict will be a stress epidemic, some academics and companies are still apparently waiting for all the evidence to be in before being convinced that stress is "real."

In our experience, there is no argument—stress *is* real. You can feel it in yourself, and you can see it in others.

Distress signals

Too much stress for too long results in visible physiological and psychological effects. You will have experienced some of these, and noticed some of them in others under excessive stress:

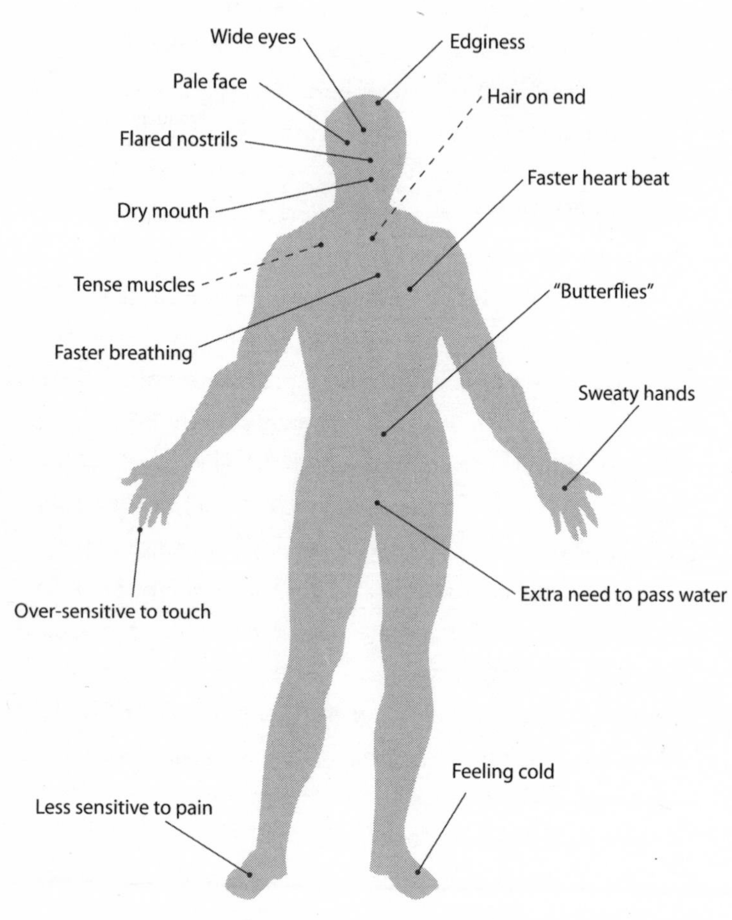

THE IMMEDIATE SIGNS OF STRESS

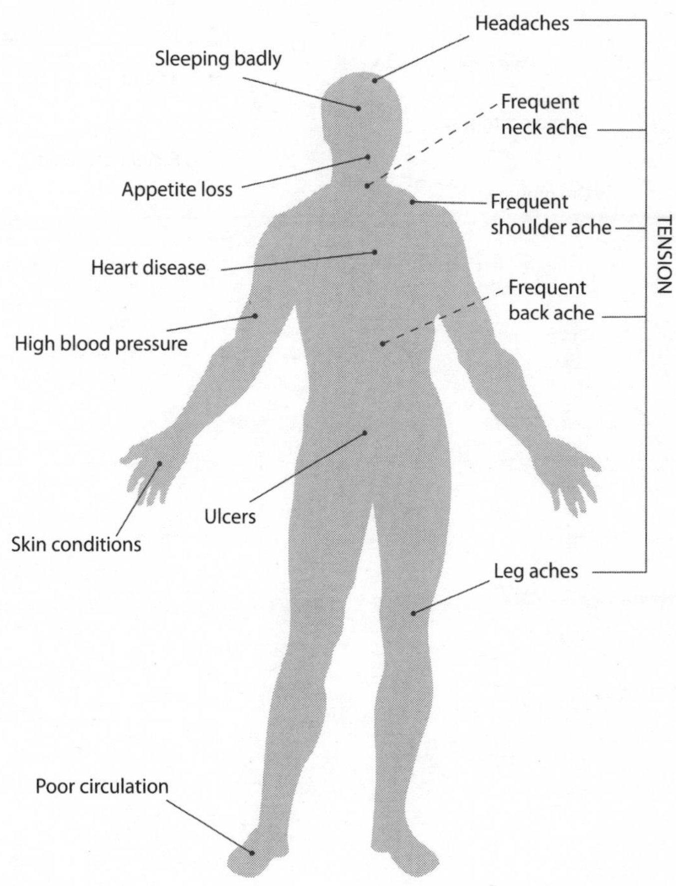

THE LONG-TERM EFFECTS OF STRESS

Stress reactions

Physical Reactions	Emotional Reactions	Mental Reactions	Behavioural reactions
Indigestion	Irritability	Inability to concentrate	Excessive drinking
Heartburn	Anxiety	Difficulty establishing priorities	Excessive eating
Ulcers	Worry	Indecisiveness	Loss of appetite
Constipation	Panic	Tunnel vision	Craving for sweet food
Diarrhoea	Depression, from mild to acute	Confused or illogical thinking	Withdrawal from people
Tiredness	Guilt	Procrastination	Clumsiness
Insomnia or poor sleeping patterns	Feeling unable to cope	Forgetfulness	Hostility
Muscle tension, aches, cramps, spasms	Heightened self-consciousness	Difficulty recalling information	Faster speech
Increased heartbeat		Preoccupation with illness	Mood swings
Palpitations			Loss of sense of humour
Headaches			Less energy
Migraine			Poor relationships at work and home
Nervous twitches			Less enjoyable life in general
Reduced resistance to illness			
Increased blood pressure			

Stress, anxiety and depression

Two of the most significant effects of prolonged stress are anxiety and depression. Anxiety is defined by the American Psychology Association as an "emotion characterized by feelings of tension, worried thoughts and physical changes like increased blood pressure." People who suffer from anxiety disorders may experience recurring unpleasant thoughts and may avoid situations simply because they "make them anxious." Physical conditions that may accompany anxiety disorders include sweating, trembling, dizziness, fast heartbeat. Common behavioural signs include checking and re-checking if something has happened, fear without any particular reason on an everyday and regular basis, panicking and feeling out of control.

Depression has been characterized as one of the most common mental disorders, and is much more than just feeling "sad." Many people have misconceptions about depression, and in organizations depression can even be stigmatized. It's important for people to be unafraid of this condition and its associated myths. Being ill-informed about it can have severe consequences. Some of the myths:

- It is a weakness rather than an illness.
- If the sufferer just tries hard enough, it will go away.
- If you ignore depression in yourself or a loved one, it will go away.
- Highly intelligent or highly accomplished people do not get depressed.
- People with developmental disabilities do not get depressed.
- People with depression are "crazy."

- Depression does not really exist.
- Children, teens, the elderly, or men do not get depressed.
- There are ethnic groups for whom depression does not occur.
- Depression cannot look like (present as) irritability.
- People who tell someone they are thinking about committing suicide are only trying to get attention and would never do it, especially if they have talked about it before.
- People with depression cannot have another mental or medical condition at the same time.
- Psychiatric medications are all addictive.
- Psychiatric medications are never necessary to treat depression.
- Medication is the only effective treatment for depression.

When trying to understand and help other people or yourself it's important to recognise your limitations and where other professionals should become involved. Identifying the difference between normal sadness, anxiety and depression can sometimes be difficult but the following symptoms can indicate the need for specialist help:

- Persistent sadness, anxiety, anger, or "emptiness"
- Feelings of hopelessness, pessimism
- Feelings of guilt, worthlessness, helplessness
- Loss of interest or pleasure in hobbies and activities that were once enjoyed, including sex

- Social isolation, meaning the sufferer avoids interactions with family or friends
- Insomnia, early-morning awakening, oversleeping
- Decreased appetite and/or weight loss, or overeating and/or weight gain
- Fatigue, decreased energy, being "slowed down"
- Crying spells
- Thoughts of death or suicide, suicide attempts
- Restlessness, irritability
- Difficulty concentrating, remembering, making decisions
- Persistent physical symptoms not responding to treatment, such as headaches, digestive disorders, and/or chronic pain[12]

Acknowledging stress

If you get stressed and at times feel over-pressured and unable to function to your normal level of capability, perhaps feeling that nothing will work out, or that you can't cope, you are not alone. Everyone gets stressed at times. Accept the fact that there are limits to what you can do within a finite number of working hours.

Understanding the processes we go through when we feel stressed is the single most important technique for managing our stress levels and the stress levels of others. Once we begin to understand the processes that cause us to get stressed, we can begin to take back control. Until this happens, most people are simply victims of an unconscious process.

Read on and find out how you can deal with pressure.

Extreme stress—a case-study

"To be identified as 'talent' in my organization, you had to tick the box 'mobile.' Only if you were 'talent' were you entitled to be in the mysterious 'succession plan' and offered an international assignment. In today's flat organizational structures, multinational companies have few other options to develop people other than to move them cross-functionally, i.e., from one department to another (for example, from marketing to sales) or from country to country. I also, unfortunately, belong to the generation where we were brought up to believe that having a big multinational name on your CV was a must if you wanted to move ahead.

"I had climbed up the corporate ladder quite fast. I had travelled around the world so much that there was absolutely no excitement left in boarding an aircraft or any glamour involved in using the airline lounge. I had conditioned myself to be able to fall asleep the minute the plane took off. Some days I would get to the evening and realize that I hadn't had any water or even been to the toilet all day. More sophisticated personal tasks such as plucking my eyebrows were forgotten. I was really exhausted, day in day out, completely overworked and in a zombie-like state.

"On one overseas placement I found myself in a country where, despite speaking the language fluently, I found it impossible to adapt. Every day around 3 p.m., I would feel tired and listless, and this triggered a habit that would soon become a real issue for me. Almost on automatic pilot, as though watching my life going by, I would leave work, head for the nearest supermarket and buy three to four kilos of chocolate, which

I would then consume in less than thirty minutes. I would burst into tears without understanding the reason why and be unable to stop. I would hate myself, feel disgusted and would throw the leftovers in the bin. Sometimes, after a few minutes, I would go to the bin to look for them and I can still remember the awful smell of the kiwi peels that were in the bin as I tried, frantically, to find the chocolate.

"No one at the office knew what was happening to me; I was an expert at hiding it and was the happy, cheerful colleague during the day.

"This went on for a few months. I hated being with people, I stopped going out, lost interest in everything and everyone. All I wanted was to be on my own in bed watching TV. My menstrual cycle was no longer regular and I had gained twelve kilos.

"One Thursday morning, the normally conscientious me just could not get out of bed to go to work. It was the first time that had ever happened in my working life. I was the type of person who would not get ill or stay at home if I did not feel well.

"It was the same on Friday. I went back to my own country to see my doctor, and, as I was waiting to see him I read one of the leaflets in the surgery and recognized my symptoms as depression and binge-eating disorder (BED). He did not want to let me go back to work but I insisted, so he prescribed me an antidepressant. I instinctively felt it was the wrong thing for me but I took it.

I went into a deeper depression, this time a 'silent' version of it. I call it 'silent' because I had absolutely no feelings of any kind—bad or good, happy or sad. I could not even cry anymore. I felt empty. For the first time in my life I would look out of my apartment window and understand why somebody would want to commit suicide.

"That's when I met a therapist who helped me get back on track, and to whom I owe my life. I gradually stopped the antidepressant and became 'alive' again. With his help I managed to fully recover.

"People ask me today if I can eat chocolate. And the answer is yes, I can! Like a normal person, I can eat a normal amount when I want to. For at least a year after what happened I felt uncomfortable because I was afraid of 'falling back' into the darkness and kept 'testing' myself. I know now that I am 'safe' because I am able to deal with things in a different and more effective way."

This case study exemplifies what happens when your unconscious takes control in order to protect you. In this case the eating disorder began as an attempt to soothe the symptoms of stress—chocolate contains "feel-good" chemicals, after all. But the effects are only temporary. The British Psychological Society (2004) defines BED as engaging in uncontrollable episodes of binge eating but without compensatory purging behaviours; these episodes are associated with eating much more rapidly than normal, eating until feeling uncomfortably full, eating large amounts of food when not physically hungry, eating alone through embarrassment, and feeling disgust or extreme guilt after overeating. Other examples of loss of control are when people turn to alcohol, drugs, or obsessive behaviours—all are responses to extreme stress.[13]

WHAT STRESSES YOUR PERSONALITY TYPE

How different personality types are stressed by different stimuli, why self-awareness matters, and how it can be developed

All of us have experienced situations where another person's behaviour causes us anxiety or distress.

There is the senior executive who is conscientious and deals well with the daily corporate stresses, but who must arrive at the office early every day to prepare herself for the unpredictable demands of her line manager.

There is the partner in a law firm who has to pick her five-year-old daughter from school, and runs the gauntlet of the same jibe, "Half day, Sharon?" as she leaves every day.

There is the manager who cares about his team and knows each of their strengths and weaknesses, and as a consequence, doesn't make demands of them that will stretch them and takes on the extra work himself.

There is the team member who feels unable to cope

because of the demands being made by the manager in charge, who never seems to find the time to offer help or even recognize she is struggling.

There is the personal assistant shared by two bosses who keeps getting loaded up with so much work but is unable to leave on time because she doesn't know how to say "no" when asked if she can do yet another task.

There is the executive who lives out of a suitcase because he is regarded as "mobile" because he has no family.

Some people need structure, with tasks well explained in advance; they need to know where they are now, where they are going and how they will get there. Others need less detail, preferring more autonomy and less guidance. Some need to feel a sense of purpose, while others are completely task-oriented and prefer a detached approach. Neither is better or worse, neither is more or less effective; these preferences just relate to how people process information, how they prefer to have information presented to them, how they make decisions, how they respond towards the external world and how they prefer to lead their lives. If their preferences are not met—at least some of the time—they start to feel pressured and, eventually, stressed.

Understanding your psychological "Type"

We have chosen to include one of the favourite personality-type theories used in Occupational Psychology, because of the practical way in which it deals with thinking styles that produce behaviour—a source of much occupational stress. Widely used in many countries, this is a valuable theory that helps individuals understand and value differences that can otherwise be sources of conflict, stress and misunderstanding whether in the workplace or at home.

Based on the personality-type theory of the Swiss psychiatrist, Carl Gustav Jung, and then made accessible to the wider public by Isabel Briggs Myers and Katherine Briggs, the Myers-Briggs Type Indicator (MBTI)[14] provides us with a framework in four dimensions to help us understand ourselves.

Assess yourself: Which type are you?

There are four questions in the following pages, each with two possible answers. For each answer, there are several statements listed under it that usually apply to people who would give that answer. Not all the statements have to apply to you for you to choose that answer—just most of them. As you read through the statements don't think too hard about them—just choose the answer that you instinctively feel most applies to you. And if both sets of answers seem to apply, ask yourself which do you do *first*?

Where do you get your energy?

Extraversion

E

- Do you get energized by external sources and stimuli?
- Do you prefer talking and being with other people over privacy?
- Do you develop your thoughts externally, i.e., through talking to other people?
- Do you prefer to have a variety of things to do, like hobbies, interests, etc., and go for breadth rather than depth?
- Are you easy to get to know? Can people usually read your emotions on your face?
- Do you tend to take initiative in social situations or at work, e.g., introduce people to one other?

Introversion

- Do you get energized by being on your own when you are tired?
- Do you prefer privacy over talking and being with others?
- Do you tend to develop your thoughts through reflection, in your own head, before you express them?
- Do you go for "depth" in things that you like to do, like in your hobbies and interests?
- Do you often "surprise" other people because they think they know you?
- Do you prefer to communicate in writing rather than over the phone or face to face?

How do you gather data?

Sensing

S

- Do you prefer anything that has to do with your five senses; facts; evidence; your experience? Do you distrust intuition and inspiration?
- Do you prefer a step-by-step approach when somebody gives you something to do or when you are dealing with a project?
- Do you prefer to live in the here and now?
- Are you quite traditional and disinclined to reinvent the wheel if not necessary?
- Do you tend to take a practical approach, go for the details, and like things to be clear and measurable?
- Books and movies—do you prefer "real-life" stories?

Intuition

- Do you prefer ideas, concepts, abstract notions, patterns and meanings?
- Do you tend to go for the big picture and get bored easily?
- Do you tend to dream of the future, of how many different options there may be? Are you good at imagining different scenarios?
- Do you tend to take a creative approach and like to come up with different ways of doing things and not want to be ordinary?
- Do you tend to skip steps when you are doing something, or ignore instructions?
- Books and movies—do you prefer science fiction?

How do you make decisions?

Thinking

- Do you tend to make decisions based on cause and effect—a logical, analytical and detached approach?
- Do you tend to look for the "objective truth"?
- Do you tend to take a long-term view?
- When you make a decision, do you tend to stick to it?
- Does the concept of "fairness" mean "consistency" to you?

Feeling

F

- Do you tend to make decisions based on your personal likes/dislikes, your values and convictions, and the impact they may have on people?
- Do you like to belong, and want harmony?
- Do you tend to empathize with people?
- Is it maybe difficult for you sometimes to say "no" because you enjoy pleasing people?
- Does the concept of "fairness" mean "taking into account each person's needs"?

What is your approach to life?

Judging

- Do you like a well-ordered life with clear boundaries and directions?
- Do you like to know at any given point where you are, where you are going, and how you will get there?
- Do you tend to plan ahead, and make decisions quite quickly?
- Do you tend to like a certain routine and make lists, plans and schedules?
- Do you get satisfaction from the completion of things?

Perceiving

- Do you prefer a more spontaneous, ad hoc, flexible lifestyle? Are you open to surprises?
- Do you prefer to postpone decisions for as long as possible because you don't want to miss out on any of your options?
- Is it quite difficult for you to decide on issues sometimes?
- Do you get satisfaction from the "journey"—the process rather than the end result *per se*?

You may have found that in some cases, you indeed could identify with both columns. That's because as intelligent individuals we learn to adapt our behaviour to different people and situations. Under stress, however, we revert to type, and do what comes naturally to us.

Knowing our type helps us understand why some people's behaviour can be annoying and stressful to us, and it transforms that behaviour from a source of conflict to a point of interest and curiosity. The same things that may be a source of motivation to some people can be a source of stress for others. Constant change, for example, can be a major stressor for J-types, whereas P-types may thrive on it and take it as a new opportunity to do things differently.

Put together the four letters that correspond to your answers above, and you will see which one of the 16 different personality types you belong to:[14]

ISTJ	ISFJ	INFJ	INTJ
ISTP	ISFP	INFP	INTP
ESTP	ESFP	ENFP	ENTP
ESTJ	ESFJ	ENFJ	ENTJ

What stresses *your* personality type?

Now that you have an indication of your Type, you can think about the things that cause *you* stress. Below, you can find a useful guide that shows potential "stressors" and "energizers" depending on your Type:[15]

ISTJ and ISFJ

Stressors

- Deadlines
- Other people's incomplete or sloppy work that affects the quality of your own work
- Being asked to change something with no good rationale provided, dealing with sudden change
- Being asked to do things in an inefficient, ineffective way
- Being asked to "wing it," brainstorm or imagine outcomes

Energizers

- Organizing facts and details to accomplish a goal
- Reaching closure before moving on to another task or project
- Quiet work space with few interruptions
- Clear and stable structures, procedures and expectations
- Adequate time and support to perform to their own standards
- Being in control of work schedule

INFJ and INTJ

Stressors

- Dealing with details, especially things in the outer world
- Working under ignorant, irrational or illogical people
- Too much extraverting
- Noisy, disorganized work environment
- Being asked to violate standards and principles
- Lack of follow-through and poor performance by co-workers

Energizers

- Flexible schedule with control over work methods and results
- Maximum autonomy
- Clear definition of role, responsibilities and expectations
- Organized, structured, predictable environment
- Co-workers who communicate directly and honestly
- Ability to achieve closure on tasks and projects

ISTP and INTP

Stressors

- Working under strict rules and regulations
- Working with, being supervised by, or supervising incompetent people
- Being responsible for or dependent upon others' work results
- Anything illogical, unjust or unfair
- Too little time alone, having to deal with too many people, being required to be extrovert
- Being confronted with strong emotions

Energizers

- Freedom to work as long and intensively on a project as desired
- Working on concrete projects with tangible results
- Having work contributions genuinely appreciated
- Being respected for special expertise
- Being included and heard in important discussions and decisions
- Autonomy and independence

ISFP and INFP

Stressors

- Multiple tasks, demands and roles
- Rigid structures and time pressures
- Conflict and hostility in the workplace
- Insufficient time to work alone
- People who are controlling and demanding or confrontational
- Political climate that demands conformity to unacceptable values or procedures

Energizers

- Work that encourages enactment of personal values
- Opportunities to help and affirm others
- Co-operative, open, congenial atmosphere
- Being appreciated and valued as an individual
- Recognition and respect for expertise and contributions to the organization
- Relaxed, flexible approach to deadlines

ESTP and ESFP

Stressors

- Deadlines
- Having to conform to a rigid routine with little free time
- Long-term planning
- Inability to control circumstances
- Vague directions and unclear guidelines
- Binding commitments with no allowance for contingencies

Energizers

- Variety and flexibility in tasks required and in use of available time
- Freedom to interact with people
- Being able to make good use of their memory for specifics
- Having options in the ways tasks are accomplished
- Clear structures, specific tasks and goals
- Working as part of a team

ENFP and ENTP

Stressors

- Having to reach closure too soon
- Being disrespected; having competence doubted
- Being overloaded with details
- Supervision that is too close and that communicates distrust and doubt
- Too little outside simulation, too little excitement about projects
- Rules that inhibit the creative process and drain energy

Energizers

- Variety and challenge
- Autonomy in accomplishing tasks
- Being taken seriously, valued for competence and special skills
- Freedom to create innovative and effective solutions to problems
- Permission to delegate implementation of solutions to others
- Adequate unstructured time

ESTJ and ENTJ

Stressors

- Lack of control over time and tasks
- Changing procedures and poorly defined criteria
- Disorganized environment
- Frequent interruptions
- Illogical behaviour
- Incompetence—your own and others'

Energizers

- Opportunity to lead and direct people
- Predictability
- Closure of tasks and projects
- Logical procedures and behaviour
- Opportunity to achieve in a well-defined, structured environment

ESFJ and ENFJ

Stressors

- Co-workers who are uncooperative, undermining
- Confrontational, divisive relationships
- Having to deal with sudden change
- Personal criticism
- Being required to treat others impersonally
- Insufficient time to do a good job
- Work that violates personal integrity and values

Energizers

- Ability to control workload and schedule
- Sociable, supportive environments
- Being valued for individual contributions
- Feeling connected to and in tune with others
- Honest and open communication
- Genuine and frequent expressions of appreciation

Hence, in practical terms, for people who have an SJ preference (Sensing, Judging), the sources of stress are likely to be things that create a lack of certainty—like change or even missed deadlines. They may "react" to these in various ways, like defining and redefining objectives, checking and rechecking, and consequently appear distressed to their teams, for example, if they happen to have the opposite preferences.

People with a preference for SP (Sensing, Perceiving) may not like to be told what to do, may get bored easily or may feel they have too few facts to work on—all of which can cause them stress. They will counter that by seeking diversions, behaving in frivolous ways, becoming resentful, ignoring advice.

As for NTs (Intuition, Thinking), who have a natural preference for variety, they may get stressed by excessive routine, too much bureaucracy, or a tight structure, and may react in a rebellious manner, or let work pile up and start being intolerant and critical.

Those with a preference for NF (Intuition, Feeling) find it stressful to deal with any kind of conflict; they don't like letting people down or saying "no"; and they get stressed by impersonal treatment. They may then start showing their feelings openly and become over-emotional.

In general, according to a research report conducted by OPP in 2006, people who have a preference for Feeling (F) tend to get more stressed than those with a preference of Thinking (T). One element contributing to this is that Feeling people tend to take things more "personally," more "close to the heart," rather than staying "detached" and separating themselves from what is happening. Additionally, people with a Judging (J) preference are more likely than those with a Perceiving (P) preference to be able to prevent stress. This may be due to their tendency to make contingency plans, and to finish their work well in advance in order to be able to deal with any potential unforeseen events.

Scrutinizing your stressors

The next thing you need to do is to act on your stressors. Look at the stressors under your personality type. Are there any additional stressors that you can think of? Add these to the list as well.

Now, for each of these stressors, rate how stressful it is for you, on a scale of 1 to 10. Once you've rated them, identify your three or four most important stressors, and consider the following questions for each one:

- Is this in your control, i.e., are you able to do something about this?
- What is keeping you from doing something about it?
- What resources do you need in order to do something?
- What do you need from other people in order to feel less stressed about this issue?
- What are the things you notice other people do that make you feel stressed?
- What are the things you can do about the things that others do?

The key is to strive for some balance if that is possible. In work or in your personal life, you are "required" to do several different activities. If all of those are "non-preferred" activities, it is bound to result in frustration and stress if done over a period of time.

Manifestations of stress for different types

Knowing your Type gives you another important insight: the ability to recognize the warning signs of stress *peculiar to your type*. By "warning signs" we refer to those changes of behaviour that crop up when you work over long periods of time, when you have to deal with competing demands, personal and professional, and so on. Even if you do notice these changes in yourself, you will often choose to ignore them, for the sake of getting your work done, most likely to a deadline. In such situations, you experience what is called "Type Exaggeration."

This phenomenon, identified by Kummerow, Barger and Kirby in 1997, posits that in stressed situations, the behavioural traits peculiar to your type manifest themselves in extreme form—you become an exaggerated version of your Type.[16]

For example, somebody with a natural preference for Sensing (S) normally "scans" his or her environment—picking up information. In the exaggerated version, under stress, he or she may become "obsessed" with just one single aspect of an issue—losing his ability to see things "in the round."

Or, for people who have a preference for Intuition (N) and who, under normal circumstances, "see connections," when stressed they may see everything as connected to everything else.

People with a Thinking (T) preference who tend to critique in an analytical way, lapse under stress into a dismissal of everyone else's views and insist on their own.

It is important to take a break when such behaviours emerge, for they are your "personalized" warning signs of stress. We sometimes don't recognize them ourselves and it is usually other people who make us aware of our exaggerated behaviour.

If these warning signs are not heeded, however, under extreme stress we can become totally out of balance, and start saying or doing things that neither ourselves nor others recognize as being in our character. We find ourselves saying things like "I really don't know how I said that" or "I can't believe that was me who did that." These are times when the parts of ourselves that we use less often come to the surface in a completely irrational and upsetting way. All Types experience these "explosions" in different ways. For example, a person at work whom we usually think of as confident and organized, if pushed to extremes over a long period of time could suddenly take a piece of criticism personally or have an emotional outburst in front of people. He would be embarrassed in front of his colleagues and they in turn would be surprised at this "unexpected" behaviour.

If and when such incidents happen to you, make sure you take a break. Do not beat yourself up or feel embarrassed about what took place. What were the things that pushed you off balance? Is there a way of ensuring that these will not take place in the future? If you happen to be with someone who is having such an experience it is not worth trying to reason with them at that point; rather, suggest to them to take a break too. They may need some space and time—ten minutes, an hour, a day or two—to deal with what happened and get back to their normal state of mind.

Understanding your Uptime and Downtime

"Uptime and Downtime" is the second concept we'd like to introduce, for understanding your own personal stressors. Whereas the MBTI is based on the understanding of your Type, Uptime and Downtime will call for you to examine the reality you live in.

Reality is a subjective experience. Even though two people may have been involved in the same "reality"—e.g., seeing a movie together or going to a party—they may have totally different perceptions and feelings about it. Our "reality" is based on the different information we have available to make sense of the world in which we live.

Sometimes people under pressure experience a strange reality. They replay events in their minds in such perfect detail that they seem to re-experience the same events, complete with all the same feelings. It is almost as though they repeat the physiological experience—sometimes again and again and again. This is a type of hallucination. When people take their work home with them they also have a tendency to take home all the events surrounding that work. By replaying these work events in their minds, they cause stress by reliving them all over again.

Downtime is the term used to describe the thought process when we think so graphically about an event—whether from past or future—that we end up having a physiological response to it that is the same as when we actually experienced it. Downtime:

- Can be positive or negative;
- Affects you physiologically;
- Will cause you harm if dwelt in for too long.

Uptime, on the other hand, is the process of staying in the present by observing what is happening around us without any associative thinking or quest to make meaning—meaning which may or may not be accurate or realistic. Uptime:

- Occurs when you experience the present, what is happening now;
- Is based on sensory information about a present experience—what you see, hear, feel, smell or taste;
- Keeps your mind off thoughts that cause stress.

Our ability to re-experience events can be useful and necessary. We can learn from past experiences and plan against their reoccurring. However, if we continue to re-experience stressful, negative events, we amplify that stress, causing ourselves harm—even becoming depressed. Feeling depressed about things that are going wrong in your life is normal. It's perfectly normal to be worried about what a pay cut may mean for you and your family; in fact you'd be a bit abnormal if you didn't feel that way. What matters is the degree to which you will think about your situation and where your unconscious or "random" thoughts will lead you before you come back to the here and now.

In the here and now, whatever is happening around us is happening. No more and no less. We are all only capable of one reality at a time. Our thoughts are both a blessing and a curse: they allow us to experience several different realities simultaneously, but uncontrolled thinking can cause us to live in doomsday scenarios, so that the reality of our present existence only becomes clear to us once in a while, and we find ourselves experiencing everything except what is happening.

Staying in Uptime

We use a technique called "staying in uptime" with our various clients. This is an exercise designed to keep thoughts in the present moment, which we insist they try for ten minutes.

Take a walk around, outside the building preferably. For that small amount of time, limit yourself to one experience—the act of walking around observing your present reality and experiencing it without engaging in any associated thinking.

The vast majority of the hundreds of people we have taken through this exercise are surprised at what they discover:

- "I never realized how many trees there were outside and I can't understand how I'd missed them for all those years."
- "I realized how I almost never stay in the present."
- "I found it really difficult and unnatural."
- "Very calm and relaxing, I felt as if I was looking at things for the first time that I'd seen for years but been unaware of."
- "Very difficult to stay in the moment, I found myself thinking about what I had to do later."

All of these comments reflect a similar idea: a recognition that we spend a great deal of time in an altered state of consciousness, separated from the here and now. Recognizing that is the key to understanding the process that causes us to spiral downwards into the depths of a despair which, once reached, are very difficult to rise above.

A person feeling depressed could walk down an ordinary street on a sunny day full of people with smiles on their faces, people with expressionless faces, shops, activity, pleasant smells, unpleasant smells, noises, laughter, beauty and ugliness—and not notice any of them. That same person could walk down the same street when not depressed and notice all of these things. The "reality" of his surroundings has not changed; only his state of mind has.

Our ability to experience other realities is actually a skill we learn from an early age—as children having to deal with boredom. As a result, we can fantasize freely when playing a game in the garden, when being driven around at night looking at the lights around us, when reading a compelling book, or when watching films and TV programmes that innocently present us with alternate realities to enjoy for a few hours at a time. These activities are harmless enough and, in fact, our ability to experience things and events other than those happening in the here and now is immensely important to our development, and is an aspect of imagination, invention and intelligence. The trouble is, we are too good at it.

Staying in uptime entails keeping out these wild imaginings, and limiting your responses to what is actually happening. Control your thoughts, and you control your feelings. This is what "uptime and downtime" gives you, the awareness that stress comes about from downtime thought processes; practise it well and soon enough you will find that without thinking certain things, making certain assumptions and going through certain thought processes, you simply can't end up feeling stressed!

To get going on increasing your uptime, try this exercise. Make a list of, say, 10 things that stress you. For each, write down whether it's one that you experience in uptime, or downtime. How many of them do your experience in downtime?

Defeating depression

Remember that of the various ways of altering one's state of consciousness, "thinking" is the most insidious. The other ways—like using alcohol, drugs, watching movies, listening to music, socializing, exercising, shopping—require *conscious* effort, and so can be consciously resisted.

Plain and simple "thinking" can lead us to altered states of consciousness that are as powerful as hallucinogenic drugs. We are not "thinking"; we are actually "experiencing" events as if they were happening and the results can be fatal.

People who feel depressed are often under the impression that they are in some way "weak" or alone in the way they feel and that everyone around them seems to be coping with their situation perfectly well. This perception is often one of the most damaging. Everyone you meet is likely to have issues, problems, fears and concerns. You are not alone—ever.

When you feel stressed about something that is not taking place, you are responding to an internal representation of an event that is no longer happening. Learn to stop this.

Finally, learn to turn your memory and imagination, when they *do* wander, to positive things. People do not get stressed by re-experiencing happy, joyful events. We can choose what we think about. Choose your out-of-body experiences consciously.

ORGANIZATIONAL CAUSES OF STRESS

The realities of trying to create a positive, productive workplace

So we now understand ourselves a little better, but what about trying to understand the organizational causes of workplace stress? Understanding the pressures and priorities of organizations and those who lead them is vital in appreciating the most common or most powerful sources of stress at work. This chapter highlights the challenges facing organizations and people-management professionals when trying to satisfy customers and shareholders while maintaining a positive, productive workplace.

Research done in 2007 by the universities of Glasgow and Paisley showed that British workers are suffering "email stress"—swamped by messages and constantly monitoring their inbox. While a third thought they were checking their inbox every 15 minutes, researchers found, using monitors fitted to computers, that they were actually checking them up to 40 times an hour. Thirty-three per cent of those asked said they felt stressed by the volume of email and a further 28 per cent said they felt driven to respond immediately to messages. This is a relatively recent "stressor" in the workplace—a phenomenon of the last 15 years—there are many more.

Categories of stress at work

There have been various efforts to quantify and identify workplace stress and thereby come up with solutions to relieve or eliminate it. Like the Lernaean Hydra, however, whenever one source is dealt with, another pops up. Stress is a subjective experience, and as we have tried to emphasize throughout this book, it is as much the product of how we generate it through our own cognitive processes, belief systems and imagination.

Workplace stress can arise in several areas:[17]

Job

The concept of "job" covers principally one's working environment and working hours.

The thing about changes like the introduction of an open-plan office is that what is seen as a positive step by so called "change-agents" could be a stressful change for the people affected. So while open-plan offices are intended to increase performance through interaction and communication, they also adversely affect people in terms of noise and lack of personal space. We have worked with people in organizations who have reported how stressful it is for them to have to find a workstation in order to be able to do something as fundamental as doing their job. We have also met people who describe a sense of homelessness and a lack of belonging because they couldn't have personal things like family photographs around them. If you're one of these, you will experience higher stress levels than you did before—negating the possible advantages of the change.

A major source of stress within this category is what constitutes a working day. The idea of "a fair day's pay for a fair day's work" has become an acceptance of long hours as the norm. In some of the organizations we have worked with, staying on long after official working hours is seen as a sign of commitment, a sign of being—or having the capacity to be—a high-performer. In uncertain economic times, people will stay behind to "show willing," to separate themselves in some way from others so that if a reduction in headcount is required, then they may have the advantage—all other things being equal.

The phenomenon of "presenteeism" is the opposite of "absenteeism." People suffering from presenteeism will come to work even when genuinely ill or when their presence is not required.[18] The driver of this behaviour is to be seen to be present, regardless of the need. Ironically, when these people leave their organizations, they are treated like anyone else who leaves: they are simply replaced by somebody else, and in time, forgotten.

So, perform to the best of your ability and continually seek clarification from management on whether you're on track. Responsible and effective managers will keep their direct reports advised of deadlines and insist on working within a working day unless the situation demands otherwise.

High-tech addiction takes a toll on the brain

In June 2010, the *New York Times* reported:

"When one of the most important email messages of his life landed in his inbox, a few years ago, Kord Campbell overlooked it. Not just for a day or two, but twelve days.

"He finally saw it while sifting through old messages: a big company wanted to buy his Internet start-up.

"The message had slipped by him amid an electronic flood: two computer screens alive with email, instant messages, online chats, a Web browser and the computer code he was writing."

Kord Campbell was not simply deluged by information, he was addicted to the constant stimulation from these multiple sources—at the expense of family and daily tasks. This resulted in a state of distraction. "It seems like he can no longer be fully in the moment," said his wife.

We, too, face this situation every day. Telephone calls, email, tweets, texts—a never-ending stream of demands on our attention. Not knowing how to manage it can lead to stress. Even though multi-tasking can give you a feeling of being productive, scientists have found that heavy multi-taskers have more trouble focussing. And this lack of focus persists even after multi-tasking ends.

So while you get a "high" from tackling these bursts of information, be wary of the enduring changes it could be making to the way you think and behave.

Workload

Managing workloads becomes increasingly challenging as organizations reduce headcount. Stress from one's inability to manage could arise from

- inefficient and ineffective use of the time and resources;
- lack of training or insufficient orientation when first joining an organization;
- lack of, or too many, processes or inefficient work flow within it;
- excessive bureaucracy.

As organizations become flatter, the need for one person to cover two positions is quite common. In many organizations, the concept of "shared services" means administrative or support functions are shared by many and we find people operating as "half a headcount," i.e., half a person supporting finance, for example, and the other half supporting HR. This leads to conflicting priorities for the person holding that position and demands a balancing act between two "power bosses."

For example, administrators in many private and public sector organizations are at the lower end of the pay-scale. In one organization we worked with, the administrators performed front-line services, interacting with the clients and ensuring the smooth delivery of programmes and services. Often, they had very large workloads and reported to more than one boss. The very genuine cause of stress they face was a massive workload high in importance and at the front end of the company, whose quality of product was judged by the professionalism of these very administrators who were overworked and underpaid.

Job role

At the job-role level, sources of stress include

- overlapping or unclear tasks or roles;
- lack of sufficient training;
- lack of effective supervision;
- imbalance between responsibility and authority;
- lack of objectives or unclear objectives;
- job title but no authority attached to it.

All of these elements affect morale and motivation, and can ultimately end in disengagement by company employees.

We've met managers who describe themselves as "eunuch managers"—they have responsibility, in theory, for certain tasks, but absolutely no authority. Their line managers in turn have none as well and the organization as a whole does not delegate. This rigid hierarchical command-and-control management style is interpreted as a lack of trust in people to do the right thing, and leaves them feeling angry, frustrated, and sometimes worthless.

Work relationships

Work relationships are many and varied and become sources of stress when the politics of mistrust occur within an organization. In our work with companies who have graduate-recruitment schemes, we've seen fresh-faced recruits become downcast with the challenge of trying to figure out how to manage upwards and sideways, i.e., their line managers and peers, respectively. As the lowest things on the food chain, finding out about the importance of relationships is crucial for their survival and longevity. Getting it wrong can mean missing out on a plum job in a much desired area.

People higher up the food chain face similar challenges with the leadership style of superiors. The degree to which they involve their employees in decision-making, the tone and channels of communication they use, how they perceive and exhibit feedback and offer recognition—are all elements that affect the climate within a department. Consider this example. The senior manager of a world-renowned blue-chip organization describes his boss as a nice-enough man, but a workaholic and a micro-manager:

"My boss by passes me and goes directly to my direct reports when he wants something done in a hurry. He does that to other department heads and it drives them crazy. When I talk to him about this and about following the chain of command, he says that it gets things done more quickly to go directly to them. What really upsets me is the fact that he has been told about his micro-managing and how upsetting his behaviour is, via 360 feedback. But since receiving that, he has simply stopped communicating with us. I think he's definitely a workaholic. He sends emails at 5 a.m. and at 11:30 p.m. He's at that time in his life when his kids have grown up and left home and his whole life is just work—a substitute for everything. I will end up just finding it too much and resigning. I feel it's already affecting my health. I never realized how important good management is until it wasn't there."

Stress: The real-life stories

In an effort to understand how organizations create stress for their employees through their structure and culture, we interviewed numerous people in senior management positions.

We wanted to identify the organizational factors that cause stress, and discover whether these individuals had ever had cause to worry about their mental and physical well-being because of work. We also asked them, in their experience, what organizations could do to diminish the effects of stress in the workplace and how they personally have been able to help their teams manage pressure.

The answers we received were refreshingly honest and rich in detail.

1 HR manager in the telecommunications industry

What are the 3 main causes of stress for you at work?

Not having a specific framework of rules, policies, procedures, roll-out of workload and prioritization. In short, not knowing what is expected of me as a person and of HR.

Lack of efficient and effective communication. The HR role is very demanding and leaves very little room for misunderstandings or miscommunication.

The current culture does not support HR initiatives and activities. Culture is the most demanding and long-term "project" within a company, and I feel that the shift towards a flexible and open culture that reinforces knowledge management is very important. However, when I'm working with strict time-frames and trying to respond quickly to achieve good results, then having to work with culture at the same time is truly very stressful.

Have you ever been worried about your mental or physical well-being as a result of pressure/stress?

Two to three years ago, I got myself into a vicious cycle that included only work, results, constant change of requirements, adjusting to those new requirements and then back to work, new results, etc. I completely lost my work–life balance, was depressed at times and could not find the strength to get out of this situation (although in general I am considered to be a strong and disciplined character with control over his life). The result was that I lost interest in and motivation for work, and my professional performance was seriously compromised.

Luckily, because I was driven to my limits I recognized I had a problem and finally decided to do something about it. I have a lot of colleagues with the same problems I had; I look at them now and they look ten years older than they really are.

In your experience, how could organizations best help people to deal with the pressures of work, change and work–life balance?

It is all about planning and organizing. When this is not evident, or not done adequately, then the leadership style of the leader of a function or department plays a vital role in how much pressure cascades downwards to his or her team.

Organizations must promote a climate of knowledge-sharing, confidence, initiative, and tolerance for mistakes; only then will employees develop a stronger immune system against stress and have less fear of change.

The terms "accountability" and "ownership" should be clearly defined—in my experience these can have distorted definitions.

Positive outcomes are expected as a natural obligation on the part of the employee and are very rarely acknowledged or rewarded, whereas negative outcomes become a very good opportunity for the employer to "build a case" against the employee. Most of the time, people avoid responsibility because they do not want to risk failure. Strong parent–child relationships in business just make this situation worse. So my advice to leaders in businesses would be: Let your kids (at work) grow up (professionally). If you don't do that, you have no right to complain about the "family" you have built.

Do you believe that in your position, you can help people in times of stress?

Yes, but it is not a matter of position as much as a matter of character. People come to me because I help them see the lighter side of things. This is something I'm comfortable doing and I genuinely enjoy it. This is not just because I'm in HR.

What HR as a profession could do is promote this type of interaction between leaders and the teams they work with, independent of hierarchical level. Some coaching in this would be helpful. Conducting training and workshops in work–life balance will not help the vast majority of people; it is still theory. Leading by example—and coaching people through their stressful issues—is the key.

2 HR director, in the tobacco industry

What are the 3 main causes of stress for you in your work?

Dealing with sudden, expected change. When the company I worked for was acquired, it was quickly announced to me that I would be the head of the human resources department in this new and bigger company. There have been a lot of changes for me to deal with—in the organizational structure, in the people, in the culture. During such times of change, HR is often "blamed" for some of the decisions taken and is the "frontline" in communication.

Maintaining the HR budget when the company is tightening budget controls. How do you defend it? How can you prove the added value to the company of investing this money?

Crystal ball gazing, i.e., guessing what might happen in the future and ensuring that people will be better prepared than the competition.

Have you ever been worried about your mental or physical well-being as a result of pressure/stress?

Even though I have been through highly stressful periods I have always managed to find ways to face them and get through them, or at least keep the worst moments to a limit. It's also a matter of how much of yourself you put into your working life—which should not, however, be confused with how productive you are. In the end, everything is about choice—even when drowning in a situation, this is usually also by choice. So, no, I have not been worried about my mental or physical well-being—I think!

In your experience, how could organizations best help people to deal with the pressures of work, change and work–life balance?

Know your people—it's important to understand the general business situation and how it might affect them, but equally important to understand that something might be happening that affects just one person or only a small team of people. It might even be something personal. The key in most cases is managing communication.

Respect an employee's work–life balance. The best thing is to make sure he has the personal time to devote where he or she chooses. I do not believe in extra "team-building" activities that go beyond office hours.

Do you believe that in your position, you have the power to help people in times of stress?

I think so and I certainly hope so! This should be a question for others to answer because in the end it's not about what you deliver but about what the other person received.

3 Senior manager in insurance company recently gone through merger

What are the 3 main causes of stress for you in your work?

Not liking what I'm doing—this was the case in my previous job, which led to burnout. I did not want to get up in the morning and go to work.

Disagreeing most of the time with the directions and goals of the company in my area of responsibility; there is no way I will feel committed and empowered to do things.

Bad relationships with supervisor and colleagues. The hours we all spend at work are long and I want to be able to feel that the relationships I have with the people I work closely with are also human relationships. If I had to work on a daily basis with someone I did not like, I would still do it, of course, and that person would never know about it, but that would exhaust me emotionally.

Have you ever been worried about your mental or physical well-being as a result of pressure/stress?

Yes, several times. That's why I decided to quit my previous job. I had several mental and physical symptoms: depression, loss of energy and willingness to do things, headaches, stomachaches, mental exhaustion, anger, anxiety.

In your experience, how could organizations best help people to deal with the pressures of work, change, work–life balance?

Have a more human approach and be close to people. Since this is usually the job of HR to initiate and maintain, have people in HR who think pro-actively and can support employees with these concerns. HR should then have the power to positively influence senior management and make sure that everyone in the organization gets the support required.

Do you believe that in your position, you had the power to help people in times of stress?

To a limited extent yes. I say limited because I was alone in this. No one else in senior management really cared about that. The company was going through a very difficult period for 18 months and zero action was taken to support people in times of uncertainty. The impression I was getting was that through this crisis, senior management and HR focused on day-to-day things more than they used to. It was as if they were locked in their offices, did what they were asked to, and avoided talking about it. Whenever I was meeting colleagues I could sense that they wanted to talk about the anxiety and uncertainty they were experiencing, and they always did that after closing the doors of their offices first. So yes, given the situation, I did my best.

4 HR manager, in the telecommunications industry

What are the 3 main causes of stress for you in your work?

1. Too much work and not enough time.
2. When the work–life balance is out of sync.
3. Not being supported by your manager during stressful projects (e.g., restructures, outsourcing).

Have you ever been worried about your mental or physical well-being as a result of pressure/stress?

Yes, when I'm stressed I tend to neglect my physical well-being (grabbing food on the go, not taking time to exercise and relax with friends). I find it difficult to relax until I know I've "completed" what I need to do (which can be hard if you're working on a stressful project for six months).

In your experience, how could organizations best help people to deal with the pressures of work, change, work–life balance?

1. Offer a 24-hour confidential employee support line.
2. Ensure managers are accessible during periods of change.
3. Ensure teams meet regularly and support one other (more likely to pick up if a colleague isn't quite right).
4. Ensure plans are transparent, and communicate regularly to agreed time-scales. If there are any delays in the process, communicate these and the reasons why.
5. Provide managers with change-management workshops to help them support their staff through periods of change.
6. Reward people for doing a good job, not for working long hours. In my organization, staying late constantly is a sign

that you are not managing your workload, so staff are strongly encouraged to leave the office on time (and senior managers do the same, making it more acceptable).

7. Senior managers should lead by example. One of the directors I support, whenever he goes on holiday, always ensures he emails his team to inform them who his deputy is, and that he won't be checking emails or texts during his time off. This sends a very strong message to the team to do the same.

Do you believe that in your position, you have the power to help people in times of stress?

I don't think HR truly has the power to help people in times of stress; I think the support largely comes from the line manager. The line manager may refer to the company policy on stress-management, advise of the employee support line, allow the employee some time off to have some breathing space, and potentially refer them to Occupational Health to ensure they are getting the medical support they need. The line manager may also recommend a stress-management workshop and follow up with the employee after this to see how they can implement some of the techniques they learnt.

I've explored coping mechanisms as part of coaching relationships; however I don't feel HR as a function plays an active role in helping employees manage stress. Currently I think this would be perceived by the business that HR was interfering.

I also feel that HR is constantly striving to become more strategic, and now feel that this is at the expense of HR playing the "employee champion" role, and supporting employees during periods of stress or personal difficulty.

5 Senior administrator at a university

What are the 3 main causes of stress for you in your work?

Having to rely on others to fulfill their roles within the team or organization. As an administrator you are often powerless to control a situation, or deliver on expectations, as this invariably depends on the input and action of others.

Unrealistic or urgent deadlines being imposed with little notice or without your knowledge.

Lack of understanding from superior reports and other organization members as to what your role entails. This can lead to a feeling of not being valued or respected.

Have you ever been worried about your mental or physical well-being as a result of pressure/stress?

Yes. If I experience too much stress I start to feel physically ill and emotionally exhausted. Trying to catch these symptoms early is the challenge.

I sought medical assistance in the form of antidepressants and talk therapy (Cognitive Behavioural Therapy).

I now voice my frustrations and concerns a lot earlier than I would have done and seek to share the responsibility of the problem or situation I am facing.

In your experience, how could organizations best help people to deal with the pressures of work, change and work–life balance?

In my experience, working in an environment where the impacts of stress are fully understood has really helped. I am lucky enough to work in a department where both of my superior reports understand and empathize with those in their departments. I have worked in organizations where this is definitely not the case and this only serves to exacerbate the feelings of stress.

Do you believe that in your position, you have had the power to help people in times of pressure and stress?

I have no power other than providing support and understanding to colleagues when I sense that they too are feeling the effects of stress.

6 Business development manager at a university

What are the 3 main causes of stress for you in your work?

1. Excessive, close-minded control.
2. Manipulation purely for self-interest.
3. Arrogant incompetence.

Have you ever been worried about your mental or physical well-being as a result of pressure/stress?

No, never—we must only allow work to be one aspect of a varied and fulfilling life. My father didn't, and committed suicide, which has always been a warning.

In your experience, how could organizations best help people to deal with the pressures of work, change and work–life balance?

Rotate the organization and associated roles to avoid hard-wiring bad habits and trapping people in ghastly situations. Recruit management with extreme care, examining their balance, particularly their ability to motivate, inspire, and to grow professionals, giving them the freedom to use natural talents in a modern world.

Do you believe that in your position, you have had the power to help people in times of pressure and stress?

Not really; only as a colleague, and in a rather discreet way, to avoid inevitable unspoken management retribution.

7 PhD, government regulatory

What are the 3 main causes of stress for you in your work?

1. Lack of interest in the job.
2. Lack of clarity from the line manager.
3. Unrealistic deadlines set by senior management..

Have you ever been worried about your mental or physical well-being as a result of pressure/stress?

There was a period last year where for months on end, I only had about 3–4 hours of sleep each night. This was due to the pressures at work and the MBA. I tried various things to relax myself but none worked. I was worried because I became absent-minded in some instances and even locked myself out twice.

In your experience, how could organizations best help people to deal with the pressures of work, change and work–life balance?

To start, ensure that they have the right people in the right place. Those who enjoy and are good at what they do will be prepared to absorb the pressure more easily.

Recognize that while it is important to set stretching objectives, one cannot operate effectively above a threshold continuously. At heart, we are human beings who need to recharge. It is perfectly normal in a business to push the limits and put in the extra hours to meet tight deadlines. However, this is not sustainable forever without a break. The onus is on line managers and their direct reports to identify the threshold and ways to recharge.

Do you believe that in your position, you have had the power to help people in times of stress?

I have done this mainly by listening to people's grievances, providing an outlet for them to vent their frustration.

8 Head of Legal Department

What are the 3 main causes of stress for you in your work?

Managing staff expectations of pay in the face of budget constraints. The lack of pay-rises makes people feel they have somehow been singled out, leading to their threatening to quit, emotional blackmail, etc. As a manager, this feels very personal and can be very wearing.

Lack of management communication and support. I had the unfortunate experience of finding myself with a manager who wasn't interested in what I did, who didn't communicate, wouldn't have meetings, take phone calls, read emails. It was impossible to know what he wanted.

Dealing with the agendas of people who are out to promote only themselves. I have a strong sense of right and wrong and am a strong team player. I expect people to treat one other with respect. When faced with such a selfish individual I struggled to cope, partly because my own sense of values didn't allow me to stoop to his level and fight fire with fire.

Have you ever been worried about your mental or physical well-being as a result of pressure/stress?

In respect of the first instance described above, coping involved doing the research, i.e., knowing how the salaries benchmark, ensuring that there was a robust and verifiable way of managing performance reviews, ensuring there was 360 feedback, etc. Then using that information to ensure that it was rigorously and objectively applied when allocating such budget as there was meant I could be confident in holding any discussions with staff and could justify the outcome knowing that although the decisions I had made were unpopular they were not made capriciously.

I also had an executive coach at one time who was able to help me with a number of very practical tools for managing the physical and emotional effects of stress, which have been very helpful in allowing me to handle those effects. Over the years I think as a result I have managed to handle a level of stress that would otherwise have caused much more physical impact.

Ultimately though, in relation to the point above the uncommunicative manager, there was only one way out of the situation and that was to leave. The person in question was the CEO so there was nowhere else to go.

In your experience, how could organizations best help people to deal with the pressures of work, change and work–life balance?

Communication, communication, communication. Change and restructuring are inevitable; if organizations are open about it, do it as early as possible and keep people up to date; they will find their own ways to cope. In my experience it is usually not knowing that people find hardest.

Do you believe that in your position, you have had the power to help people in times of stress?

Managers may be constrained by various organizational forces, but at the very least, you must treat people with respect. That is key.

PART 2
MANAGING PRESSURE & STRESS

5 TAKING CONTROL

Techniques for mastering your internal condition and your responses to stressful situations

A high-profile female corporate lawyer has a fear of turtles and tortoises. She rationally explains that her fear is only of the "really big ones." As she describes her fear, she manifests the physiology of a phobic response: sweaty palms, increased breathing rate, flushed neck and cheeks, general agitation. If she continues to talk about turtles much longer, she could ultimately reach "switch-off" point and pass out. She knows logically and rationally that unless they sneak up on you unnoticed, turtles and tortoises pose little or no threat even if they were to get close to you. That includes the Giant Tortoise, which would rather eat a lettuce than you.

Your unconscious mind

A phobia isn't the product of the "conscious" mind—that logical, rational, analytical mind that can dissect scenarios and cases with forensic skill. A phobia is the response of the "unconscious mind," which has information about turtles that has yet to be updated from the time the phobia was installed, which was probably between the ages of one and seven.

Regardless of intellect, people with phobias, who can construct solid rational, objective arguments for a living, cannot convince their own unconscious that something should no longer be feared. This is because the general rule governing these two consciousnesses is that if there is a conflict between the conscious mind and the unconscious mind, the unconscious will always win.

Knowing something about the unconscious mind is useful when it comes to managing pressure because many of the unconscious processes we use, when unchecked, cause pressure to become stress.

Many people will know someone with a phobic response to something. Common phobias are fear of spiders, wasps, flying insects and birds. Less common ones are fear of bats, cats and chewing gum.

Phobic responses are installed between the ages of one and seven. Children do not know how to fear things as they simply do not have the information to allow them to. They only have two intrinsic fears, one of falling or losing equilibrium, and the other of loud noises; they are unafraid of spiders, cockroaches, worms, fire, razor blades, scalpels, open log fires, pots of boiling water and oil. Parents live in mortal fear of their children's fearlessness at times.

A spider phobia is typically installed when a child approaches a small black unfamiliar shape moving along the floor and proceeds to investigate it with all its senses, and a parent or sibling—someone bigger and older—on seeing this lets out a cry (loud noise), rushes forward, swiftly lifts the child (loss of equilibrium), and carries him away from the offending creature to safety. This double whammy installs a response, held within the unconscious mind, that is reproduced consistently well into adulthood, and is quite baffling to a rational person who tries to explain it rationally.

Phobias are a dramatic display of how we can respond to an unconscious process. When we stop the process the response ends. And to stop the process, the first step is to become self-aware.

Self-awareness is the key to taking control

There are two main ingredients in any stressful situation—the external sources of stress, and our internal conditions:

- External sources of stress can be our job, our relationships with other people, our home situation and all the situations, challenges, difficulties and expectations we may be facing at any time during our lives.
- Our internal condition is made up by our nutrition, our overall health and fitness levels, our emotional well-being, the amount of sleep and rest we get—all of which determine our body's ability to respond to, and deal with, the external stress-inducing sources.

Managing stress involves, therefore, making changes in the external conditions we face, and in the internal conditions which strengthen our ability to deal with what comes across our daily paths. There are many things we can do to help ourselves regain control over both these sets of conditions and it is our responsibility to take action when we detect signs of stress in ourselves or others.

In this chapter, we will show you techniques for taking control of your internal condition. The techniques need reflection and commitment to work but their effect can be profound. They need to become part of your life on a regular basis, so that you are aware of how you have arrived at a particular state of mind and the process you used to get there.

Take control of the language you use

Changing the way you use language is one of the most powerful tools for managing your internal condition.

Check your meaning

Words are labels for things and experiences. In order to understand what another person is saying, we have to access our understanding of particular words they might use.

Each person will have his or her unique way of interpreting what a word means depending on their experience of that particular word. This process happens very quickly. With words that refer to emotions or states, people will access the times when they too experienced the same states. The effects of powerful descriptions can be quite dramatic. Have you ever noticed how when you comforted someone who felt depressed or worried, after half an hour of talking to them you felt as bad as they did? This is because we make meaning of language by accessing our understanding of each word as well as the experience they describe. People in the caring professions often need to talk to their supervisors about this phenomenon.

Consider the word "comfort"; ask yourself what this means to you personally. What is your experience of that word? To some it may mean sitting in an armchair with a glass of Scotch by an open fire on a cold winter's evening. To others it may mean curling up under a duvet, snug and warm, watching TV, or being with people that make them feel safe. People will put different labels on their experiences.

Words that can describe things differently are called nominalizations. Examples of nominalizations are:

Comfort	Panic	Anger
Peace	Love	Understanding
Happiness	Success	Relaxation
Resourcefulness	Strength	Anxiety

Nominalized speech patterns are frequently found in political speeches where the words can be taken to mean something generally positive but say nothing specific, for instance: "If I were elected I would ensure the continued growth of individuals by enabling people to use resources in new and different ways." While this may sound generally constructive and positive, it leaves many questions unanswered and is very unspecific. People who knowingly use nominalizations rely on the fact that people will supply their own positive interpretations of positive nominalizations and not ask for specifics.

The things people say to us can induce a state of anxiety and stress if our reaction to the words they use is based on a negative interpretation of their nominalizations. An important part of controlling stress is to check if our understanding is correct before responding to what we think has been said. Reacting to something someone has said when you are consciously aware of their intent is quite different to feeling agitated or negative without knowing why. You may find that certain people rub you the wrong way—it may not be due to any intent on their part, sometimes it could just be the way they use words, or the way you interpret them.

Many interactions and relationships have been affected by the use of words which have different experiential meanings. Think of your own experiences where you have thought you understood what someone meant yet got it completely wrong. Don't be a victim of responses that occur at an unconscious level—it's useful to check if someone's meaning is the same as your interpretation before responding.

Choose positive language

People often tell themselves not to get upset, not to get angry, not to worry. We think and give ourselves instructions using language; some people talk out loud to themselves while others only do this when no one's around.

However, the best of intentions sometimes receive the complete opposite response. Have you ever said to someone or had someone say to you, "Don't get angry about what I'm going to tell you..." and then you proceed to get angry? The reason is quite simple: you have been primed to do exactly what the speaker doesn't want you to.

Don't think of a blue tree.

As you read those words, what did you have to do in order to follow the instruction? You would have had to think of a blue tree first and then delete it. When you tell someone not to get angry, they have to think of anger first and then not think of it. As anger is a strong emotion, and that person accesses their experience of it, they will access the accompanying state very quickly—you will have him or her primed and ready to feel the very emotion you did not want.

We often tend to give instructions in this way, and even though we mean well, we produce a negative response in our audience. Notice how you feel when someone says:

Don't worry about what I am going to say...

Don't feel depressed...

Don't get upset...

Don't get annoyed...

Don't panic!

So, rather than say "Don't worry," just tell the person what you have to say. Rather than say "I don't want you to get angry," just say what you have to say and allow the person to have the response they are entitled to.

The language you use to yourself is as important as the language you use to others. We often instruct ourselves to feel something or not to feel something. Walking around saying "I must stop feeling stressed," will not help you to stop. Instead, say, "I must start relaxing."

As an exercise, make a list of phrases often used at work—by you or others—that are positive in intent but which produce and perpetuate a negative state, e.g. "Let's try not to get hung up about..."; "Nothing is going right...."; "I wish you wouldn't be so...."

How would you word these differently to avoid using the negative?

Take control of the state you are in

The mood or state you are in can often mean that some tasks are more easily completed than others, or that some interactions go better than others; sometimes it can mean the difference between success and failure. When our moods are not suited to the task, even things normally easy or well within our capabilities seem tedious and difficult—resulting in stress.

Learning is an area that is very often dependent on the state we are in at the time. Think of how you learnt best at school, for instance. How would you describe the mood or state in which you learnt the most? Were you relaxed and alert, or did you learn best when you were apprehensive and curious? No one learns or takes in information when they are bored and restless. Studies have shown that learning is "state-dependent" and that we learn best and quickest when we are in the best state.

During the course of a normal day, we all go through a series of states, which are either caused or influenced by other people, changing environments, words, clothing and many other things. Your state will affect others and change *their* states.

When people change mental states they also show physiological signs, such as changes in skin tone and colour, changes in breathing rate, changes in voice tone (louder, softer, higher pitched, lower), and changes in body movements.

Being aware of your own state at any given time will enable you to take positive steps to be in the most useful and resourceful frame of mind for any situation. To analyze the state you are in, ask yourself these questions:

1. How would you describe it? Is it a relaxed state, or an agitated one? Describing a state requires you to pay attention to the way you feel inside—many people are familiar with the feeling of "butterflies" that describes anxiety of some description. Being in love is an example of a powerful internal state that can allow us to feel cocooned in euphoria despite whatever else might be happening around us. In this state, even the most boring meeting could be made quite tolerable if you daydreamed about wandering off with your partner somewhere or planned your next meeting.
2. Is it appropriate for the task at hand?
3. What would be the ideal state to be in? What would you need to think of in order to access it? The ideal state to be in for a competitive athlete is one of confidence, one that can be accessed by thoughts of previous successes, as opposed to thoughts of previous losses. The ideal state to be in when approaching someone for help and support would be to access thoughts of previous times you met supportive and understanding individuals who listened to your requests fairly and openly, rather than the times you were denied a fair hearing.
4. What state are others around you in, and have they affected your internal state?

People have a tendency to wander around in whatever state of mind happens to have been produced by the last interaction they've had or the last series of thoughts and associations, often quite haphazardly. Thoughts are not random; we can direct our minds, without too much effort, to things that will change our state to suit the circumstances.

Take control of your "logical levels"

When British Rail was being privatized in 1994–97, a team of us took 168 of their managers through a change-management programme. At the beginning of every three-day workshop, we would begin introductions by asking a simple question of each participant: "What do you do for a living?" We asked it wondering if we would get a *behavioural* reply along the lines of, "I work as an accountant in British Rail Business systems," or, "I am a manager in ticketing," or, " I work in Engineering." Such answers would have told us about the behaviours they engaged in to earn a living. But instead of this, almost 85 per cent of them, regardless of gender, replied, "I am a Railwayman."

Identity-level identification

What we were witnessing there was the phenomenon of *identity-level identification* with one's work—a phenomenon with far-reaching consequences. The Railwaymen showed an exceptionally high level of commitment to the railways and the job. We also subsequently found out that many of the people we worked with were indeed Railwaymen, who had parents (often both) who worked for the railways and expected that their children would follow in their footsteps and join the railways. They took the job very personally.

Operating at the level of identity is the highest of the five "logical levels" identified by the anthropologist, Gregory

Bateson,[19] and expanded upon by Robert Dilts. Each level indicates what may be important to a person in a particular context, or the general level of information that interests the individual:

1. Environment
2. Behaviour
3. Skills and abilities
4. Beliefs and values
5. Identity

Each level is more abstract than the one before it but also has a greater degree of impact on an individual.

People who work at an identity level take their work personally and often give a level of commitment that would cost considerably more than they are actually paid. They often work hours that are far longer than contracted and they have a level of conscientiousness that can border on obsession. They often rise in organizations due to their fervour and willingness rather than their skill and abilities; this in turn can create another stress factor and often does. People who work at the level of identity often think that those who do not share their work ethic are not committed. People who work at the level of identity often take criticism of their work personally and are unable to separate their behaviour at work from themselves and consequently can react badly to change.

Which is why our group of British Rail managers reacted badly to change: because when they were told that their jobs were going to change, they heard the message that *they* were going to have to change. There is a significant difference between being told your job description is changing and that you yourself must change. The unconscious melding of one's job and one's identity has profound implications. Insurance companies in the UK are able to statistically prove that the majority of British males link themselves to their job at identity level and that this linking affects them when they retire; in fact, statistically, they start to die. Think of it this way: If you are what you do for a living, and your living ceases to exist, what happens to you? You cease to exist, that's what.

Line managers and people in HR who are used to handling restructuring or redundancies know from experience that employees who are "company people" and who identify with the organization in this way are devastated by the fact that that same organization has abandoned them. They are affected as much by this as they are the by the potential consequences of loss of income. In fact, until they are able to recover from that perception, they may not be able to re-enter the job market.

One UK company, recently acquired by a European firm operating in the same business, faced significant restructuring due to an excess of people in the new parent company, and set about advising employees that there would be a reduction in the number of engineers required, and that the positions left would be advertised and they would in effect have to apply for their own jobs. Some people were quite philosophical about it, while others couldn't understand this approach at all. To those who worked for the company at an identity level, this approach was a veritable betrayal of a personal contract. They had given themselves to the company and at quite a deep level; they had taken away time from their families, gone beyond the call of duty and invested of themselves in the organization—it hurt.

In contrast, at another programme we ran, one rather senior figure among the group suddenly shouted out that he didn't need to be on a three-day psycho-babble change-management course. He proceeded to advise us that if he didn't like what was happening, he would look for another job and simply leave, but he didn't need to whine about things for three days before doing so. He, like many other people in organizations, worked within the above model at the *level of skills and capabilities*. When people work at this level, they are quite clear about the contract they have entered into. They are happy to work hard and give 100% effort between the times they have agreed to work and also give "above and beyond." However, they are there because they have the skills to do the job, and it's skills that they are selling, not themselves. When faced with change they will be more inclined to think first in terms of their skill-sets rather than personal loyalty, although they can be very loyal as well. Generation Y is typical of this level—they want a fair day's pay for a fair day's work, and prefer trading skills and competencies rather than loyalties.

Tackling issues at the right level

Often, we experience stress because we do not know what the problem is and we confuse what area of our lives it concerns. The British Rail managers were not under pressure and stress because of the "change" they were experiencing but because they felt they were losing their identity. The majority of them were going to be doing exactly the same jobs; only their titles and the name of the organization would change. The engineers' sense of betrayal resulted from the personalization of an impersonal event—a company merger, no more, no less, and certainly not personal.

When we look at issues or problems that affect us, our view is usually dominated by the level at which we tend to "operate," and in the workplace we are quite consistent in where we choose to concentrate. As a result, we can often be blinkered to the fact that the issue may not be in the area that we think it is in, and may, in fact, be a lot easier to solve.

The levels at which we operate are mainly unconscious, but this model provides us with a framework that enables us to become conscious of them. This tool can help you establish what is important to you, what you need at work, and whether or not those needs are being met. You can assess whether you are in "alignment" with your needs, and understand why you have been anxious or stressed even though many of your needs are in fact being met.

1. What is the issue or problem? Name it specifically.
2. Is this problem at the level of the environment? Is this about your place of work, home? If so, what can be done to change it?
3. Is this problem at the level of behaviour? Does it involve other people doing or saying things, or not doing or not saying things, and if so, what can be done to stop or start these? For example, to address a blame culture—you need to start giving praise. Is it about your not being able to say things? Our behaviour includes the actions we take and the ways in which we interact with others, such as working as part of a team or working more as a loner.

4. Is this a problem at the level of skills and abilities? Does this involve inadequate training or a feeling of lack of competence which can be addressed by providing skills training? Is this about your own capabilities and how you perceive them?
5. Is this a problem at the level of belief and values? Does this involve conflict between what you and others think? Why do you think this is an issue? Do others hold the same beliefs as you and have the same problems? What can be done about this?
6. Is this a problem at the level of identity or role? Is this specific to you? Is this an issue linked to your role or job description? Would it be an issue regardless of your role or job?

By taking time to think about an issue and reflect on what we can do once we have identified it, we can sometimes find a way forward ourselves or seek appropriate help from others.

Take control of your negative thoughts

Imagine you have invited a friend to come to your house and they are late and haven't called. Do you think "How typical of them! I knew I could not trust them!" Consider what could be some of the feelings associated with this interpretation of the particular event? Probably disappointment, anger, bitterness, confirmation of some of our insecurities. However, if we thought, "They are probably stuck in traffic and I am sure they will be here soon," the feeling associated with this interpretation would be optimism, leaving us more in control.

We as human beings are extremely good at making

assumptions and arriving at conclusions all the time. We search for patterns and continuously try to make meaning of events and people. Most of the time we are not even conscious that we do it. Indeed our survival at times can depend on our ability to reach these conclusions—the ability to do so is in fact a sign of intelligence.

However, the negative consequence of this ability is that once we accept something as fact—be it about others or ourselves—we tend to ignore any evidence that would support the contrary. Children, for example, who are told by a parent that they are "useless," grow up looking for evidence to support this statement—which had been merely directed at a specific act. These are "dysfunctional assumptions" or even "destructive core beliefs" that affect the way we behave and act.

What if an employee has a core belief that "I am a failure"—how would that affect his relationship with, say, his line manager, who in the course of work will be giving him feedback both positive and negative or, as they are commonly called, "areas for development"? Instead of taking this constructive feedback the way it is intended, our employee will choose to take it personally, to enforce his belief of being a failure, and thence proceed into scenarios that involve what happens to useless people who get found out for being useless and how ultimately nothing works and so on and so forth. The reality of the situation is that what has just taken place was a performance-management discussion, quite common and usually quite mundane, with surprisingly few variables. However, our employee has had another version of reality.

Cognitive Behavioural Therapy (CBT)

How can we eliminate these "negative automatic thoughts"—as the American psychotherapist, Aaron Temkin Beck, calls them? Beck believes that people can be retrained to alter the way they think, and unlearn thinking habits that are not helpful at all. It is by doing so that we can ultimately change the way we act.

This, in essence, is the basis for the therapeutic framework called Cognitive Behavioural Therapy (CBT), which Beck was instrumental in developing in the 1960s. CBT focuses on the present instead of the past—the here-and-now instead of the skeletons in the closet. Research shows the effectiveness of CBT in treating conditions like depression, social phobia, anxiety, panic disorders, obsessive-compulsive disorders and eating disorders. Because it is easily accessible, is based on a particular skill set, has a proven track record of success, and can produce results relatively quickly, CBT is increasing in popularity.

What is CBT?

Cognitive Behavioural Therapy helps you learn a healthier, more useful style of thinking. It gives you a way to change the way you think ("cognitive") and how you behave ("behavioural") as a result of this thinking pattern. The focus of CBT is on the "here and now" and what you are telling yourself in the present, instead of issues that may have caused you distress in the distant past.

It works through breaking down a problem into parts as

shown in the following diagram, to make it easier for you to address the problem. The underlying assumption is that each of the parts in the diagram affects the other. So, a situation will produce a certain thought, the thought will evoke possibly an emotion, which may result in a physical feeling, and all this will produce a behaviour.

SITUATION » THOUGHTS » EMOTIONS » PHYSICAL FEELINGS » ACTIONS

When we attribute blame to another person for making us feel something, we have responded to something they have said or done. The feeling we end up with is not the direct result of what they have said, but what we have done with their words through our thoughts. Our thoughts have caused the feelings and subsequently the way we behave after they have said what they have.

For example, someone who says something to you in order to let you know how they feel such as, "I wish you had not done that," is designed to let you know exactly that. It is possible however, to take that simple sentence and work on it to such a degree that you feel aggrieved or depressed by the end of a thought process that will include thoughts of unfairness, how the tone of voice reminded you of someone else who had been horrible and unfair to you, and so on. How you feel the event is going to impact your life is not necessarily the same as the event itself.

This can be a vicious circle that can actually make you feel worse. CBT can help you break this vicious circle of altered thinking, feelings and behaviour.

(Source: Royal College of Psychiatrists)

Take control of the "truths" about yourself

Some of the most seemingly confident people often have nagging doubts about themselves despite having years of proof that they are more than up to the job. These doubts fall into what we call the "according to me" category—they are the subjective "truths" we have about ourselves *that we maintain even in the face of overwhelming evidence to the contrary.* You can challenge the validity of your own "according to me" truths by using the following exercise.

First, identify the issue that troubles you:

- Am I competent enough?
- Am I part of the team?
- Am I being included?
- Am I needed?
- Am I doing a good job?
- Am I liked? What do people think of me?
- Am I being rewarded/acknowledged?
- What will happen next?
- What are my prospects for the future?
- How many steps will it take for me to progress?
- How clear a career path do I have?
- Where do I go from here?
- Does my line manager care about my progress?
- How can I be sure I am safe in restructuring?
- How can I be sure I am on track?

Next, ask yourself these three questions with regard to the issue in question:

1. How do I know? What is my evidence procedure?
2. What do I need to know?
3. How much of an issue is this, on a scale of 1 to 10?

Example: *Am I competent enough?*

1. How do I know? What is my evidence procedure?

My performance appraisal ratings; feedback from my line manager; feedback from my team.

2. What do I need to know?

What are the standards of the organization I work for? What are my line manager's expectations?

3. How much of an issue is this, on a scale of 1 to 10?

I would rate it a 3—hence may not be as important compared to other issues.

The difference between what is *given* and what is needed is what will cause stress and pressure. Needs are a question of degree. Are they realistic? Reasonable? Do you know this? Do others know this? The difference between what you need and what others are able, willing, inclined to give equals to pressure.

Rate yourself, in what areas do you need to decrease your rating?

TAKING ACTION

A practical guide to reducing your stress on a day-to-day basis

Self-awareness needs to result in action for it to be useful. One of our regular clients asked if their trainer could shadow us and run managing pressure courses for the organization's lower levels. Twelve months later she was signed off work having suffered a breakdown. She had run back-to-back stress-management courses without taking her own advice on rest and recuperation.

Looking after yourself requires you to take action.

Looking after yourself at work

Since the workplace is the source and scene of most of the stress we face today, it is the best place to begin making changes:

- Adopt a positive and appropriate way of communicating—the responses you get will depend a lot on the way you approach people.
- Have clear objectives and make sure you know what is expected of you.
- Ensure you are working within your competence level and ask for help or training if you need it.
- Adopt realistic work practices. Good managers try to help their people and while there always will be times when the "pressure is on" and everyone is working beyond their normal pressure zones, this can be unsustainable over a long period.
- Look after your own well-being. Remember that you do have limits and that as you inhabit a physical body, you must take breaks, eat, drink, rest.
- Build positive relationships with others and avoid anything that might damage your relationships with people.
- Be open to feedback from others and give good quality feedback in return.
- Get some fresh air. Modern office buildings have controlled atmospheres—fresh air is great for Uptime. In many of the organizations we work with, people who smoke look after their mental states by taking frequent breaks (obviously they harm their physical health by smoking) and are often observed with disdain by their colleagues who continue to sit at their desks and PCs for hours on end till they are reminded by their bladders to take a break.

- Reward yourself. What do you need to do to acknowledge your own efforts? Rewards often help to convert drudgery to work. Find something to reward you and only you—as opposed to your being pleased because others are pleased—there is a difference.
- Avoid working excessively long hours and taking work home. If you find yourself doing this ask yourself why and assess whether it is really necessary.

Dealing with information overload

- Immediately get rid of "useless information," e.g., adverts in your email.
- Organize your inbox; label incoming mail according to priority and urgency.
- Get rid of instant notifications and avoid responding to instant messages and emails immediately. Set aside specific times to address these messages during the day and limit the number of times you address them. People will eventually figure out when you are most likely to respond.
- Try setting aside some time on a regular basis to catch up with people. In this way you will less likely be interrupted during your work hours.
- Try "disconnecting" after a certain time. Technology today allows us to take our work to bed, to the WC, literally everywhere. The Blackberry has rightly gained the nickname "Crackberry" to signify people's addiction to these devices.

- Set aside time for reading the news, and filter the sources in a strict manner
- If you are one of those who subscribe to every single newsletter, blog, etc., ask yourself: Do you really need all of them?

Looking after yourself at home

- Listen to relaxing music in surroundings where you will not be disturbed for at least half an hour.
- Consider some form of relaxation—yoga, meditation, massage, tai chi, aromatherapy—then do it.
- Take regular exercise each week. This counteracts the negative effects of stress and is a good way to build resilience. Any exercise is better than no exercise at all; walk part of the way to the office or take a neighbour's dog for a walk in the evenings. Book a regular lunchtime or weekend walk with a friend—exercise and socialize at the same time.
- Ensure you have adequate sleep each night. The body needs approximately eight hours to repair itself. There are several simple steps that can be taken to improve your quality and quantity of sleep:
    - » Sleep as much as you need to feel rested; do not oversleep.
    - » Avoid forcing yourself to sleep.
    - » Try to stick to a regular bedtime schedule.
    - » Avoid drinking caffeinated beverages—tea, coffee, soft drinks—later than the afternoon, and definitely avoid nightcaps—alcoholic drinks prior to going to bed.

» Avoid smoking, especially in the evening.
» Avoid going to bed hungry.
» Ensure your bedroom has the appropriate environment—light, noise, temperature.
» Try to leave your worries outside the bedroom.[20]

Watching your diet

- Eat sensibly. Keep your body supplied with sensible amounts of food so you can maintain necessary energy levels.
- Avoid eating sweet snacks; these give short-term energy but in the longer term make you feel tired.
- Drink plenty of water throughout the day. Tiredness is a common sign of dehydration; the body needs two litres of water daily to be fully hydrated.
- Avoided caffeinated drinks such as tea, coffee and cola. Caffeine dehydrates and acts as a stimulant, raising stress levels.
- Alcohol, cigarettes and drugs may give you a short-term boost but have well-documented long-term health effects. Consider other ways to boost your energy and concentration.

Give yourself time

Now, give yourself some time and—if you've made the right adjustments to your life as suggested above—things may soon fix themselves.

Research within the psychotherapeutic setting by Miller,

Duncan, and Hubble, *Escape from Babel* (1997), attributed 40 per cent of the success of treatment to what happens outside the sessions.[21] This means that events in the outside world which were beyond the therapist's or client's control were a major part of the success. How often have you made a decision to buy or do something and found out that if you'd waited just a little longer, you would have been able to get an even better deal or seen a better opportunity? Often the things we set in motion do not come to fruition as quickly as we'd like and impatience prompts another action. Learn to implement a change in behaviour or thought and philosophy—and give yourself time. Falling in love, making a new friend after going to a party you never wanted to attend, getting a promotion, being chosen to help someone as a mentor, being contacted by someone from your pleasant past, all fall into the category of what happens on the "outside."

Remember that suffering in silence is self-imposed. It may also be self-defeating, as individuals making claims against employers will be unsuccessful if they simply front up to their boss or the company and try suing them for stress; test cases have shown that the courts believe there is an obligation on the part of the claimant to tell the employer that they are stressed so that they are given the opportunity to do something about it. The more help you seek, the more likely you are to overcome what's bothering you and troubling you.

Whatever it is, don't lose hope. Hope is the way we allow the possibility of something happening to us that will change our situation positively. Nothing is hopeless. Even if you don't see any hope, it is because the state of mind you are in prevents you from seeing it; it doesn't mean there isn't any.

What do pressure-free or less-stressed people do that others don't?

1. They have a well-developed self-awareness.
2. They are informed.
3. They are open about how they feel.
4. They communicate and talk about their issues.
5. They have interests and activities outside work and nurture them personally.
6. They check that their expectations are realistic and achievable.
7. They measure themselves at work around skills and capabilities.
8. They eat and sleep properly.
9. They know about the system within which they work and live (reasonable expectations of employees and job).
10. They are self-aware (we know it's already been mentioned but it's worth mentioning twice).
11. They realize that unless they actively take part in monitoring, evaluating and taking a pro-active role in their own well-being, they cannot expect others to be mind-readers.

BALANCING THE ORGANIZATION AND THE INDIVIDUAL

How to prevent stress in your organization, and what to do when it arises

In 1998, we were asked to conduct a stress audit for a large engineering firm, a move prompted by concerns that four of the firm's engineers had been forced to take time off due to nervous breakdowns. The organization was male-dominated, and the macho corporate culture meant that although there was no explicit position on stress in the workplace, if there had been one, it would no doubt have been along the lines of "stress is for wimps." This unspoken attitude was partly responsible for the breakdowns of the four engineers—they hadn't recognized the signs of stress or felt able to address them. They did not have a way of knowing they *were* stressed.

We have also met managers who were horrified when members of their team went off sick due to stress. They genuinely had no idea that the person was at the point of being unable to cope.

Managing stress within the corporate world is a two-way process. Employees need to be able to realize that they are stressed, and then to tell someone, hopefully their line managers, that they need help. Managers need to be able to recognize that often the people most likely to suffer from stress are their most conscientious team members and that stress is a very real condition.

Human-friendly management?

Gary Hamel, author of *The Future of Management*, says, "We live in a world today where you can't live, where you can't win unless you get the very best out of your people—and it turns out that probably for the first time since the Industrial Revolution, you can't build a company that's fit for the future unless you build a company that's fit for human beings. Isn't it odd that our companies, our organizations are less human than we are? Let's just admit it—management that's been practised for the last 100 years has not been very human-friendly."[22]

Hamel points out that in the world of technology we have seen staggering advances such as the microchip, the internet and the unravelling of what makes us human—the human genome—yet what comparable advances have we made in the field of management?

The answer is probably very few indeed. But this book does not seek to put forth new management theories; it is intended to highlight the need for individuals to take care of themselves by being more aware of themselves and the areas that cause pressure. Stress can result in people absenting themselves and

Modern management

Management practice is fundamentally about organizing human beings to achieve tasks. In an effort to look after our shareholders, our clients and the people who work for the organization, we try to please everyone.

The techniques of modern management started with the approach formulated by F.W. Taylor in the early 20th century (subsequently called "Scientific Management" or "Taylorism") and was originally intended to stop workers consistently under-producing on the machine-shop floor. Taylor was a machine-shop foreman.

Taylor represented a shift in thinking for his time and believed that the way to stop under-producing was to

- systematically (or scientifically) compile information about the work tasks required;
- remove workers' discretion and control over their own activities;
- simplify tasks as much as possible;
- specify standard procedures and times for task completion;
- use financial (and only financial) incentives;
- ensure that workers could not deceive managers, or hide from them.

Many agree that jobs in many modern organizations (perhaps most) are based on Taylorism and that scientific management enables organizations to grow and prosper, but that says nothing of the mental health of the people in them.

in labour turnover. This will in turn increase pressures within a business area and become self-perpetuating.

Recognizing the signs of stress

Teams can benefit from recognizing the signs of stress in members. In an atmosphere of openness where myths surrounding those who suffer from stress are dispelled, recognition is the most positive first step that can be taken.

Consider some of the warning signs:

Within a business area:

- Increase in labour turnover
- Complaints and issues raised at exit interviews
- Feedback from surveys or meetings
- Increases in issues regarding discipline or grievance

Individuals:

- Decline in performance
- Loss of motivation
- Unnecessary mistakes
- Poor decision making
- Deterioration in planning and control of work
- Emotional outbursts
- Tension and conflict between colleagues
- Complaints from clients and colleagues
- Loss of commitment or motivation
- Working increasingly long hours for diminishing returns
- Erratic or poor time keeping
- Sickness absence

To detect stress, it helps to know the different areas in which it may arise. The Health and Safety Executive (HSE) identifies seven sources of potential stressors in an organization:

1. **Culture**: What is the organization's "cultural" attitude to stress and pressure? How supportive is it of people under pressure? Is the support offered by way of counseling or confidential service simply paying lip service to a legal requirement or a genuine attempt to help. Does the organization operate transparently and try to spread the load and enable people to seek support from their colleagues? Does the organization have a culture that really believes that stress is for wimps?
2. **Demands**: How is workload determined? What physical hazards are there? The demands of the job can entail working to deadlines at short notice. For single parents, this can often be a pressure that is hard to bear as well as to physically manage. Finding support at short notice is hugely stressful, just as walking out of a meeting can be when you simply have no option.
3. **Control**: How much say do people have over their work? How does this compare with others?
4. **Relationships**: What are relationships between colleagues and departments like? Is bullying or harassment an issue? How are people managed? Is power being used responsibly? Is favouritism being substituted for merit?
5. **Change**: How is change managed and communicated within your organization and your team?

6. **Role**: How well-defined are roles within the organization? Are there conflicting roles?
7. **Support**: What kind of support is available? Are factors unique to the individual being recognized?

Burnout—a case-study

Peter is a successful and highly qualified executive working in a large, well-known international organization. With a young family and a working wife (also in a high-profile, demanding job), he had to balance his role as a loving, caring father and husband while contributing to the best of his ability to the success and well-being of his company—a familiar challenge to many.

He felt that things were going quite well at work, and while coping with personal pressures and work is never easy, he was finding the balance between the two tolerable. He felt that the personal sacrifices he was making would be acknowledged. The company he worked for had a reputation for being demanding but fair. "The stretch was worth it because it would look good on the CV," he said.

However, his mid-year and end-of-year performance appraisals revealed something else.

"The difference between the value I thought I'd given and the acknowledgement I received caused me a great deal of stress. My manager had moved on and an interim manager took his place. He ignored me. Then another interim came and in two years I had five bosses.

"The fact that there was no obvious step to promotion was not a stress factor—I just felt depressed when I thought about all I'd given up, especially time with the family. The workload was increasing and we had less resources. I was very irritable, it was very stressful and I felt my health was in danger. I didn't feel I was valued or recognized.

"I have moved on now. I care a bit less. I suppose I am delegating more (or passing it on). I'm not as on top of things, not bothering to know all the issues. I've turned the passion down, really. I have had to learn to ignore people and their requests. You can't do everything—'they' have to ask me three times now or I won't do it."

Helping someone under stress

More often than not, people under stress try to maintain a "normal" appearance and act as if everything is OK. Managers who think that someone might be dealing with an undue amount of stress should engage with that person to discover how best to help them. This is easier if the manager already has a level of rapport that allows them to ask open and honest questions and get honest replies. In this situation they will be better able to empathize, they will know how that member of their team responds under normal circumstances and be more aware of changed behaviours. If this does not already exist it needs to be quickly established.

The discussion process broken down, involves:

1. **Rapport**—the connection that allows the interaction. You know when you are in rapport with someone when certain things are "in place"—things that are important to us and we become consciously aware of more by their absence than

by their presence. Those things include knowing that someone is really listening to you and giving you their full attention; a certain amount of eye contact that indicates sensitivity and concern; verbal clues that tell you they are following what you are saying and focused on your meaning. In short, they are paying attention to you, and you respond by paying attention to them.

2. **Empathy**—the ability to understand what another person might be going through. Empathy is not the same as having someone agree with you or tell you that you're right. It's about being able to understand why a person might feel a certain way about a situation or someone's behaviour and allow them to have the emotion. After all, you may have been in a similar situation.
3. **Calibration**—the measurement of present responses against what is observed to be "normal." Within a therapeutic setting clinicians gather information about clients so that they can offer guidance and assistance. They need to gauge fairly quickly how the client manifests their comfort zones in terms of what they feel comfortable talking about, for how long, and to what level they are prepared to go with the discussion. This is called calibration. Calibration takes place within many other settings: People who negotiate, parents, doctors, partners and many other groups are experts at calibrating responses within their relationships. Calibration requires sensitivity to our

interlocutors' facial expressions, movements, tone of voice, choice of language, and emotions.

So, having established rapport, created empathy and calibrated and heard the employee explain how they feel, the manager puts them in touch with resources to help them—and then what? How to prevent the situation happening again? And what can the organization do to help all employees live "more lightly" within it?

Taking responsibility—what managers can do

Experience and working with organizations shows us that they tend to adopt "reactive" approaches, i.e., dealing with symptoms of stress, *after* they have had an incident, like a nervous breakdown, instead of having programmes in place to prevent them and educate employees. A typical reaction is introducing a training programme in managing pressure which covers just one aspect of the whole issue and yet shifts 100 per cent of the responsibility to the employee. It also gives the covert message that the organization is not going to change and that it's the employee who needs to learn how to manage himself or herself in this environment. A pitfall of this approach could also be that the individuals who really needed this training may not be attending since they have to volunteer for it. As we pointed out earlier, not all individuals are aware that they are stressed or they only find out when they are already at the end of their tethers. Others are afraid that if they do attend, this may look bad in their training and development records kept by HR and may even affect their prospects for promotion.

If you manage people, what actions can you take right now to help prevent stress and alleviate pressure? As mentioned in Chapter 4 the sources of stress are many and hence the approach that managers or the organization as a whole should adopt should also be at many different levels:

- At an **organizational level**: Adopt an appropriate management style, and clear and on-time communications, especially in times of uncertainty, like mergers and acquisitions.
- At the **job level**: Analyze jobs, workflow, processes. Sometimes organizations have gone overboard with downsizing, or with confusing matrix organizations and reporting lines. Clear roles and responsibilities minimize conflicting demands.
- At the **individual level**: Be realistic about career development and career opportunities—how many opportunities are there in today's flat organizations? Provide adequate training when employees join the organization or when employees assume new roles or when they get promoted. Provide programmes to improve employees' self-awareness and personal effectiveness; cover aspects of time management, preferred working styles, motivation, aspirations, setting expectations, becoming more effective, managing upwards, etc.

Many organizations have also introduced "wellness programmes" that offer a range of support, such as advice on how to adopt a healthier lifestyle which includes nutrition, exercise, hotlines where employees can call anonymously and discuss their concerns with experts, etc.

The following list is the result of one company's successful attempt to improve the quality of employees' lives after it was successfully sued by an employee for stress. The owners of the firm only found out about the case when they read about the judgment in the tabloid press. As a result they gave HR unlimited power to fix the problem. Staff surveys subsequently showed a major turnaround in satisfaction following the implementation of the following:

- Keep all of your team informed of any changes.
- When setting targets and objectives, keep your team informed of progress.
- Monitor the hours your employees work. Regular long hours are no good for the individual or team.
- Ensure you have a plan to meet your business objectives and involve your team.
- Make yourself approachable.
- Ensure job descriptions are up to date.
- Have regular personal development reviews with your team so they can map their progress.
- Deal with issues of discipline or grievance fairly.
- Support the individual and team with development and training
- Always ask HR professionals for help if necessary.
- Contact Occupational Health for advice if you have concerns about someone's well-being.

Organizational issues—seeing both sides

For the many issues that crop up in organizations, we list below the ones we've encountered most often. Whether you are facing pressures at the workplace or having to manage workers who are facing pressures, these diagnostics will help you identify, understand, and treat the sources of stress.

Poor relationship with line manager

Symptoms: Avoidance of contact, "managing by ignoring," acting as if the person doesn't exist.

Causes: Lack of effective communication, lack of management training, poor delegation, possible overload of line manager due to dual or conflicting roles, fundamental error of attribution, reacting to imagined scenarios instead of real ones.

Cures: Get into Uptime, ask for an opportunity to resolve things, improve communication, check possible opposite MBTI Types, set clear objectives from both sides, check your facts. What basic assumptions are you making? Does everyone have the same problem with this individual?

"Everything's a chore!" or "I don't want to go to work!"

Symptoms: Mistakes on the job that would not happen under normal circumstances, lack of focus, no initiative, passive resistance, passive hostility.

Causes: Unclear career path, being in the same position or job for a "long" period of time, lack of clear objectives, having a role but not the responsibility or authority that needs to go along with it.

Cures: Check your expectations: Are you being realistic? Are you expecting to be given opportunities without showing willingness? Is this even about work.

Lack of engagement

Symptoms: Doing the minimum required, working by the book, adopting a rigid approach.

Causes: Disappointment from performance appraisal, loss of faith in company's values.

Cures: Disappointment is allowed, not all things work out the way we hoped; expectations vary—some are unrealistic, so check yours.

High voluntary employee turnover

Symptoms: Good people leaving, talent walking out of the door.

Causes: Lack of effective induction training, lack of management.

Cures: If exit interviews are not telling you why, patterns are likely to give you the answers.

"I can't cope with this—too much work and now we have less people to do the same amount and even more work."

Symptoms: Lack of motivation, chronic fatigue.

Causes: Absenteeism.

Cures: Concerted effort by manager and team to talk realistically about priorities and help and support for each other in achieving tasks.

"How do I get identified as "Talent"?

Symptoms: Uncertainty over self-worth ("Am I one of the chosen?"), cynicism, low morale.

Causes: The company making a big deal of the latest buzzword "Managing Talent," which went from the McKinsey banking crash world of the "War for Talent" to "Keeping Talent."

Cures: HR needs a clear strategy for articulating the criteria used in this very difficult-to-explain concept. Most HR will answer the direct question of, "Am I considered to be part of this Talent thing?" by defining the criteria. Being identified as Talent is more about attitude and relationships than skills and is a very subjective process.

Being micro-managed

Symptoms: Demands for daily updates, incessant meetings, disregard for reporting procedures, bypassing line-management structure.

Causes: Insecurity of the manager, simply not knowing how to perform a managerial role. A micro-managing manager also probably scores highly on MBTI Sensing and Judging preference and needs to know where they are in relation to objectives continually.

Cures: Coaching, mentoring, 360 feedback.

"Oh no, not another training course!"

Symptoms: Cynicism, non-participation, contagion of course participants by the cynics in the group.

Causes: Training provided is too conceptual and not practical enough, or relevance of the course to job scope not clearly explained.

Cures: If courses are compulsory, HR must be explicit in their expectations for people to make the most of it. Save money by sending people who are willing to learn. Don't waste money on people who already think they know.

Workload

Symptoms: People not prioritizing, managers indicating that "everything" is urgent and important.

Causes: Lack of clear job descriptions, overlapping or conflicting work objectives, lack of adequate training, reduced resources, unrealistic demands by managers, too many chiefs.

Cures: Managers can be clearer about priorities, have the confidence to describe what is urgent and important and the consequences of not doing. Managers must know who does what in their team, and how to monitor and measure performance.

"I'm afraid of opening my email inbox."

Symptoms: Avoidance of correspondence, huge inbox with lots of unanswered mail from various sources, breakdown of communication.

Causes: Many people use email as a way of "having dealt with it"—because they have sent you an email, it's now your problem. Others just copy you and everyone else in out of courtesy.

Cures: Recognize that there are those that if unanswered or acknowledged, will damage your reputation. Even less important people who complain, can affect your reputation. If the content is personal, it's important. If it's from your boss, it's important. If it's from a client, it's important. Practise "skimming" to quickly establish what fits into which category. Everything is important until it's not.

"I've got a new position and I really don't know what to do, I am learning on the job."

Symptoms: Getting involved in things that others are already doing well, reverting to what you know how to do rather than what you ought to be doing, finding displacement activities, interfering for innocent reasons that will be interpreted as controlling.

Causes: Organizations often promote based on the excellence of a person in their current role, not their next one. People go for the next role because it offers more money and status, not necessarily because they know how to do it.

Cures: Give yourself time to be clear about your responsibilities. Find out the behavioural meanings of words like "strategic," "managing cross-functionally," "measuring work"—whatever terms your position uses to describe itself. Get coached or mentored.

"I'm not good enough; others appear so confident."

Symptoms: Unwillingness to participate, fear of going to events where behaviour will be evident for all to see, anxiety from having to be in the limelight; mortification at the thought of public speaking.

Causes: Our view of ourselves is based on how we view others' behaviour and how well we compare against those whom we approve of. Self-esteem is about how you esteem yourself against your personal criteria.

Cures: Before you accept your own judgement of not being good enough, check your criteria and ask yourself, "According to whom?" For example, our view of confidence is Western-based; in other cultures, this same behaviour would not necessarily be aspired to.

"I work very hard here, I do everything I am supposed to, how do I succeed and get ahead?"

Symptoms: Working even harder and longer to get noticed, frustration, cynicism, burnout.

Causes: The metrics organizations use to measure performance, such as having certain skill-sets or amount of hours billed, are not the metrics used to promote or get ahead.

Cures: Become aware that what makes the world go round is relationships. Two people of equal skills and capabilities will often only be separated by their attitude and their ability to form relationships.

"I hate conflict."

Symptoms: Avoidance of engagement, compromises for the sake of expedience at the expense of quality.

Causes: I hate conflict, I avoid confrontation, I don't like it when people get emotional.

Cures: What you attach to an interaction will determine your approach to it. In conversation, deal with issues rather than personalities.

"I can't motivate others and this makes me look like a bad manager."

Symptoms: Poor 360 feedback, poor achievement of goals, little teamwork, a department of individuals.

Causes: Goals without feedback—this produces a lack of commitment and the goals are consigned to the not-interesting, not-tangible bin.

Cures: Learn to set goals and give feedback to gain commitment and demonstrate your commitment as well. Studies show plenty of evidence to support the link between the achievement of goals and feedback.

"I'm working in a different culture and I don't know the rules around here."

Symptoms: Overly tentative behaviour, overly brash behaviour, perceived arrogance.

Causes: Insufficient guidance by HR and people who know the ropes. Usually through lack of knowledge transfer due to inadequate planning and lack of time.

Cures: Just showing respect for the foreign culture will ensure forgiveness for ignorance of what often is tradition. It pays to make sure you know about the most fundamental and unforgivable cultural faux pas, as there will be at least a couple.

"I don't feel I am being treated fairly."

Symptoms: Undercurrents of hostility, possible masked petulance, working even harder to redress the balance in the hope of being treated fairly.

Causes: Perceived inequity and inequality in rewards or treatment or amount of attention the person receives. Sometimes a person's performance can increase and be perceived as motivation when it is in fact an effort to restore the balance of perceived unfairness. Management can be surprised by the sudden resignation of a valued employee for the same reason.

Cures: Clear reward structures. The clearer people are about them, the less perceived injustice or effort under sufferance there will be.

FINDING SUPPORT

Where to find professional help—from financial advisors to HR to doctors—and what they can do for you

Many of the people we have met on our managing pressure programmes have come on them as a last resort and often are sent by their line managers. Many have had breakdowns before attending. We are consistently reminded by them that they did not know where to turn or how to get support when they felt stressed and pressured and guilty for feeling that way. If you are still feeling that you need help having already learnt about the ways that you can help yourself, the following tables will provide a useful guide:

MENTOR

Who: A more senior, more experienced person, who has "been there, done that"—someone who has already trodden the path you are about to embark on and can share the secrets of their success. Mentors can either still be at work or retired.

Issues they can help with: Work-related advice; sharing of experience, examples of what was done in similar situations in the past; sharing of contacts and network which might help you progress.

Where, when, how often: At work. Can continue over many years, on either a formal or informal basis. Sometimes part of a specific work initiative, with a fixed time-frame, such as senior managers mentoring graduate intakes.

How they can help: Informal, face-to-face or telephone conversations, which may be specific or general. These can go quite well depending on rapport. Confidentiality is important, so discuss this first.

LINE MANAGER

Who: Immediate superior. For personal issues or more serious work-related issues such as allegations of bullying, a third party may be requested to be in attendance by the person with the issue. This will often be a member of the Human Resources department. The individual with the issue is legally entitled to have a colleague or friend of their choice present at such a meeting if moves into disciplinary territory.

Issues they can help with: Work-related issues (e.g., problems with or complaints about another member of staff), and personal issues (e.g., absenteeism due to alcohol problems or child-care problems).

Where, when, how often: In the workplace; either informally or by formal appointment. A private room is required and should be requested if not offered.

How they can help: The majority of well-intentioned line managers will offer support up to the limits of their capability. Not suitable if they are the source of your pressure and stress.

HR

Who: The appropriate organizational representative for the particular type of issue you wish to address.

Issues they can help with: Work-related issues linked to performance or behaviour. More serious than issues taken up with the line manager—part of the escalation process in an organization. Could be also a resource for information, such as details of how to access work-provided counselling service.

Where, when, how often: In the workplace, in the HR department. Often a one-off, or small number of meetings.

How they can help: HR tries to bring an issue down to what is possible within a work setting; however, they are hence limited by their corporate remit.

COACH

Who: Either an in-house or external coach. Preferably someone formally trained in coaching, and with accreditation. Membership of a recognized professional coaching body also desirable.

Issues they can help with: Work-related or personal. Coaches focus on moving from a present "stuck" state, to a future state where a desired goal will be achieved.

Where, when, how often: A contractual relationship, over a mutually agreed number of sessions. Either organized through the organization, or by an individual for themselves. Frequency also by mutual arrangement, typically once every 6–8 weeks, more frequently if the specific issue being worked on requires it.

How they can help: Coaches can be informative and helpful in expanding your range of options through various techniques. Confidentiality is inherent in their contract with you and with the organization.

COUNSELLOR

Who: Counselling is also an officially regulated profession. A counsellor should have formal training and be a member of the counselling professional body in the country in which they are working. They should be in supervision.

Issues they can help with: "Out-of-control" emotional issues, such as bereavement, personal relationship issues, acute traumatic experiences, distress. Usually used to deal with a response to a specific event.

Where, when, how often: May take place in the work environment, in a formally designated set-up, or outside of the workplace, at a time mutually agreed on by both parties. A series of, say, six weekly sessions is normally arranged as a counselling intervention. Tends to be much shorter-term than therapy.

How they can help: Counsellors provide a confidential support mechanism, questioning and listening to problems.

THERAPIST OR PSYCHOLOGIST

Who: A formally trained therapist, with appropriate qualifications from the therapeutic field they represent. Check that they have membership of the official professional body for that therapy. Therapy is an officially regulated profession, unlike coaching or mentoring.

Issues they can help with: Deep-seated issues held at an unconscious level, outside the control of the individual at a conscious level—i.e., willpower alone will not enable change to take place. Work is done on the client's early experiences in order to change the way in which they perceive their life. Therapists can also help with chronic, disempowering issues or states of mind.

Where, when, how often: Outside the workplace, usually in the therapist's professional premises. Outside work hours, or in specifically arranged timeslots, similar to a visit to the doctor. As often as the specific type of therapy requires—usually once a week, and can continue over a number of years, e.g., psychotherapy.

How they can help: Via a range of different psychological models and interventions, such as CBT. Completely confidential with strict ethical boundaries.

DOCTORS

Who: Formally trained and qualified practitioner. GP or specialist. Some organizations will have their own arrangements with health practitioners for their staff.

Issues they can help with: Physical or mental health issues.

Where, when, how often: Doctor's premises.

How they can help: Doctors can be relied upon to help you with the physical manifestations of pressure and stress. They can also refer you to other health professionals and prescribe drugs to help you get through things.

FINANCIAL ADVISORS

Who: Formally trained and qualified practitioner, such as an accountant. Either part of the organization, or by private selection, e.g., a personal financial advisor. Check credentials and membership of appropriate professional body, and preferably use references from other people whose judgement you trust.

Issues they can help with: Financial issues such as mortgage repayments and impending redundancy, decreased earnings, unforeseen financial difficulties.

Where, when, how often: Practitioner's premises, or designated workplace sessions, e.g., with company pensions advisor.

How they can help: Various methods for controlling budgets, restructuring payments; mortgage advice.

YOUR BANK

Who: Bank manager, or business advisor.

Issues they can help with: Overdrafts, loan repayments, mortgages, credit cards. How can you make the most of your present circumstances and be prepared for what may be around the corner?

Where, when, how often: As often as necessary; banks can sometimes provide advisors to help manage your account.

How they can help: As for financial advice.

CONCLUSION: MANAGING IN THE LONG TERM

How to take charge of, and stay committed to, your lifelong well-being

Stress and pressure can be managed—and dramatically reduced—by making a commitment to look after ourselves. Indeed, the onus is firmly upon us to do this rather than on others to stop stressing us.

The sooner we understand this, the easier it is to take steps to do something about it. We take a strong and directive approach to people on our pressure-management courses and our central message is: Take care of yourself, look after your own mental well-being—it's your responsibility.

Waiting till you get ill before you take steps to look after yourself is very much like locking the stable door after the horse has bolted, but it is the most common approach that people take. Most people only become aware of their mental well-being and start to look after themselves when it has been affected—usually quite scarily and dramatically.

You're responsible for yourself

The law is quite clear in the UK: An employee is expected to be able to cope with the normal pressures of the job. If he claims to be suffering harm from mental stress within the work environment, are there signs that *others* are suffering as well? In the majority of organizations it will always be the case that there will be a wide range of responses to the job simply because pressure is also an *internally* generated response, based on what happens inside you to what happens outside you—this applies all the time, for everyone, everywhere.

In the case of *Hatton* v. *Sutherland* (2002), the Court of Appeal laid down a set of practical guidelines to follow in considering injury claims arising from work-related stress. These guidelines made it very clear that every person in the workplace has a duty to look after themselves, and that being responsible for your job and being loyal to your company also requires you to be responsible to yourself and for yourself. Conscientious people please note.

The guidelines in effect state that an employer has to be pro-active rather than re-active in looking after the mental health of employees. So long as they provide a confidential advice service with referral to counselling or appropriate treatment services, they are unlikely to be found in breach of a duty of care. Furthermore, a company would not be in breach if the only reasonable and effective way to stop a stressed-out workaholic employee from continuing to work would be to sack them. Neither are they in breach of their duty of care if they allow a willing employee to continue doing his or her job.

The Court of Appeal also made clear that there are no special mechanisms within the law that apply to claims for psychiatric injury arising from doing the work an employee is required to do, and that the "threshold question" is whether or not this kind of harm to the employee was "reasonably foreseeable."

No occupations should be regarded as intrinsically dangerous to mental health. An employer is entitled to assume that an employee can withstand the normal pressures of the job, unless he knows of some particular problem or vulnerability.

The only way an employer is likely to know this is if you have volunteered the information, and most prospective employees will not have done this, quite reasonably fearing that if they had, they wouldn't get the job in the first place.

Nor is it the responsibility of an employer to make searching enquiries of an employee's mental health. So we're back to the fact that looking after yourself is up to you.

While the guidelines have no statutory force and each claim is still dependent on its own facts, lawyers in the UK nevertheless generally advise against claiming against an employer, or, at the very least, advise on how difficult it is to establish and succeed in a claim.

The lessons learnt

It is virtually impossible and practically speaking, undesirable to live without pressure. Without a certain amount of pressure, many things would not get done. Pressure is often a way of describing *the need* for things to be done—some are more urgent than others and often the longer they are left, the greater the pressure.

1. Take some time to assess yourself. Most people sacrifice *themselves* before they sacrifice anything else. Compare your holiday self to your work self and note what is the difference and how far you are away from a totally relaxed state. See if you're OK with this as your threshold may be high and you can cope with the pressure.
2. Find out through regular check-ups with your doctor how your health is generally—you should be doing this anyway!
3. If you already have a diagnostic such as the MBTI referred to in Chapter 3, read it again and make a note of what your preferences are and how strong they are. Become self-aware.
4. By doing step 3 you become aware of what you need and the judgements you might be making unconsciously about the world and other people and what your energizers and stressors are.
5. Case-studies and other people's experiences help to put our lives and thoughts in perspective. As you saw in Chapter 4, many people share your challenges. Feeling alone is a stressor and need not be the case.
6. At a personal level take time to monitor yourself, monitoring your thoughts and taking control of them. Notice your internal state and be aware of how you got there—you can control this. Reread Chapter 5 on how to do so.

7. At a work level Chapters 6 and 7 have offered advice and suggestions on how you can improve the 21st-century workplace and avoid its many pitfalls.
8. If you need support, go out and get it. If you feel it is not possible to do it within your organization, then go outside and get it. The tables in Chapter 8 summarize the various avenues for doing so.
9. Take responsibility for yourself. We ask you to make a commitment to do something for yourself before stress forces you to.
10. A corporate commitment to helping people is equally important and those at the top of organizations are the key to driving and supporting people who work at every level in the organization.

My commitment to myself

You owe it to yourself to look after your own health, and make sure that pressure and stress don't get the better of you. Don't put it off. Start right here, right now:

I, ___________________________, having read this book, as of ____________________(date), commit to the following:

1. I will be self-aware, and monitor my physical and mental well-being.
2. I will take breaks when I am at work and will not wait until my bladder is bursting before I stretch my legs.

3. I will be conscientious about my work, and put in 100% when working and shut off when I am not.
4. I will remember to use the techniques I have available to me to relax.
5. I will check in with myself to find out where I am on my own continuum between being relaxed and stressed then I will take the necessary steps to ensure I only work at peak stress levels for the amount of time I am able to.
6. I will talk to my line manager if I need help or feel overwhelmed, and accept that this is simply part of managing oneself, and that managers must know you need help before they can help—they are not mind-readers.
7. I will remember that it is conscientious people who suffer from stress because they are always concerned about others, the company and their own performance.
8. I will remember that being too conscientious or being over the top with it can cause ill health.
9. I will remember that the onus is on me to look after myself. Suffering in silence allows no one to do anything about it, and presenting anyone with the cumulative results of long periods of stress is presenting them with a problem that could have been fixed easily earlier on.
10. I will remember that the macho attitude that "stress is for wimps" is an outdated approach and is nonsense—it is the conscientious people that suffer most from stress.

11. I will seek medical advice or the advice of health professionals if I need to.
12. I commit to referring back to this book from time to time so that I can monitor my commitment to looking after myself.

Signed ______________________

Date ______________________

Notes

1. "Wave of staff suicides at France Telecom," *Guardian*, 9 Sep 2009.
2. Russell H. Fazio, Mark P. Zanna & Joel Cooper, "Dissonance and Self-Perception: An Integrative View of Each Theory's Proper Domain of Application," *Journal of Experiential Social Psychology*, vol. 13, issue 5 (Sep 1977): 464–479.
3. Leon Festinger, *A Theory of Cognitive Dissonance* (Palo Alto, CA: Stanford University Press, 1957).
4. Rob Goffee & Gareth Jones, *Why Should Anynone Be Led By You? What It Takes To Be An Authentic Leader* (Boston, MA: Harvard Business School Press, 2006).
5. This includes cost of absence, replacement costs and lost production. However, if indirect costs such as reduced customer satisfaction and lower productivity are included, these costs would escalate substantially. "Less Stress, More Value," The Henderson Global Investors 2005 Survey of Leading UK Employers, www.henderson.com/content/sri/publications/reports/workplacelessstress.pdf.
6. Graph adapted from Robert M. Yerkes & John Dillingham Dodson, "The Relation of Strength of Stimulus to Rapidity of Habit-Formation," *Journal of Comparative Neurology and Psychology* 18 (1908): 459–482.
7. Stephen Williams & Lesley Cooper, *Managing Workplace Stress: A Best Practice Blueprint* (Chichester: John Wiley, 2002).
8. *Steadman's Medical Dictionary* (1982), cited in Valerie J. Sutherland & C.L. Cooper, *Strategic Stress Management: An Organisational Approach* (New York: Palgrave, 2000).
9. John Arnold, *Work Psychology: Understanding Human Behaviour in the Workplace*, 4th ed. (Harlow: Pearson Education Limited, 2005).
10. Daniel Goleman, *Emotional Intelligence* (New York: Bantam Books, 2006).

11. T.H. Holmes & R.H. Rahe, "The Social Readjustment Rating Scale," *J Psychosom Res* 11 (1967): 213–18.

12. "Depression causes, symptoms, treatments," MedicineNet.com (Apr 2010) www.medicinenet.com/depression/page2.htm.

13. British Psychology Society, *Eating Disorders: Core interventions in the treatment and management of anorexia nervosa, bulimia nervosa, and related eating disorders* (National Clinical Practice Guideline Number CG9, 2004).

14. Isabel Briggs Myers, *Introduction to Type*, Sixth Edition (Oxford: OPP, 2000).

15. Naomi L. Quenk, *In the Grip—Understanding Type, Stress and the Inferior Function* (Palo Alto, CA: CPP Inc., 2000).

16. Jean M. Kummerow, Nancy J. Barger & Linda K. Kirby, *Work Types: Understand your work personality—how it helps you and holds you back, and what you can do to understand it* (New York: Business Plus, 1997).

17. C.L. Cooper & J. Marshall, *Understanding Executive Stress* (London: Macmillan, 1978.)

18. C.L. Cooper, "Hot Under the Collar," *The Times Higher Education supplement*, 21 Jun 1996.

19. Gregory Bateson, *Steps to an Ecology of Mind* (Chicago: University of Chicago Press, 1972).

20. "Is sleepiness hurting you?" emedicinehealth (Jan 2010), www.emedicinehealth.com/script/main/art.asp?articlekey=112703.

21. S.D. Miller, B.L. Duncan & M.A. Hubble, *Escape from Babel: Toward a unifying language for psychotherapy practice* (New York: Norton, 1996).

22. Gary Hamel, *The Future of Management* (Boston: Harvard Business School Press, 2010).

Bibliography

Arnold, John. *Work Psychology: Understanding Human Behaviour in the Workplace*, 4th ed. Harlow: Pearson Education Limited, 2005.

Bandler, Richard. *Using Your Brain For A Change*. Utah: Real People Press, 1985.

Bandler, Richard, & John Grinder. *Patterns of the Hypnotic Techniques of Milton H. Erickson, M.D.*, Volume 1. Cupertino, California: Meta Publications, 1975.

Bandler, Richard, & John Grinder. *Reframing: Neuro-Linguistic Programming and the Transformation of Meaning*. Utah: Real People Press, 1982.

Bateson, Gregory. *Steps to an Ecology of Mind*. Chicago: University of Chicago Press, 1972.

Beck, Aaron T. et al. *Cognitive Therapy of Depression*. New York: The Guildford Press, 1979.

Berne, Eric. *Transactional Analysis in Psychotherapy*. London: Souvenir Press, 1993.

Bossons, Patricia, Jeremy Kourdi & Denis Sartain. *Coaching Essentials: Practical, Proven Techniques for World-Class Executive Coaching*. London: A&C Black, 2009.

British Psychology Society. *Eating Disorders: Core interventions in the treatment and management of anorexia nervosa, bulimia nervosa, and related eating disorders*. National Clinical Practice Guideline Number CG9, 2004. www.bps.org.uk

Chopra, Deepak. *Ageless Body, Timeless Mind: The Quantum Alternative to Growing Old*. New York: Harmony Books, 1993.

Chrisafis, Angelique. "Wave of staff suicides at France Telecom." *The Guardian*, 9 September 2009.

Cooper, C.L. "Hot Under the Collar." *The Times Higher Education supplement*, 21 June 1996.

Cooper, C. L., & J. Marshall. *Understanding Executive Stress*. London: Macmillan, 1978.

Cox, T., & C. Mackay. *A Psychological Model of Occupational Stress*. Paper presented to The Medical Research Council, Mental Health in Industry, London, November 1976.

Croyle, Robert T. & Joel Cooper. "Dissonance Arousal: Physiological Evidence." *Journal of Personality & Social Psychology*, 45, pp. 782-791, 1983.

Earley, P. Christopher, Soon Ang, & Joo-Seng Tan. *CQ: Developing Cultural Intelligence at Work*. California: Stanford Business Books, 2006.

Erickson, Milton H. *Creative Choice in Hypnosis*, Volume IV. New York: Irvington Publishers Inc, 1992.

Eysenck, Michael W. *Simply Psychology*, 2nd ed. Hove & New York: Psychology Press, 2008.

Fazio, Russell H., Mark P. Zanna & Joel Cooper. "Dissonance and Self-Perception: An Integrative View of Each Theory's Proper Domain of Application." *Journal of Experiential Social Psychology*, Vol. 13, Issue 5, pp. 464–479, September 1977.

Festinger, Leon. *A Theory of Cognitive Dissonance*. Palo Alto, CA: Stanford University Press, 1957.

Festinger, Leon, & James M. Carlsmith. "Cognitive Consequences of Forced Compliance." *Journal of Abnormal & Social Psychology*, 58, pp. 203–210, 1959.

Goffee, Rob & Gareth Jones. *Why Should Anyone Be Led By You? What It Takes To Be An Authentic Leader*. Boston, MA: Harvard Business School Press, 2006.

Goleman, Daniel. *Emotional Intelligence*. New York: Bantam Books, 2006

Hamel, Gary. *The Future of Management*. Boston: Harvard Business School Press, 2010.

Havens, Ronald A. (ed.) *The Wisdom of Milton H. Erickson: Human Behaviour & Psychotherapy*, Volume II. New York: Irvington Publishers Inc., 1996.

Hawkins, Peter, & Robin Shohet. *Supervision in the Helping Professions.* USA: McGraw-Hill, 2009.

Holmes, T.H., & R.H. Rahe. "The Social Readjustment Rating Scale." *J Psychosom Res* 11 (2), pp. 213–18, 1967.

Houston, G. *The Red Book of Gestalt.* Enfield: Airlift, 1993.

James, Tad, & Wyatt Woodsmall. *Time Line Therapy and the Basis of Personality.* Capitola, CA: Meta Publications, 1988.

Kring, Ann M., Gerald C. Davison, John M. Neale, & Sheri L. Johnson. *Abnormal Psychology.* New York: John Wiley, 2007.

Kummerow, Jean M., Nancy J. Barger, & Linda K. Kirby. Work Types: *Understand your work personality—how it helps you and holds you back, and what you can do to understand it.* New York: Business Plus, 1997.

Lancaster, Lynne C., & David Stillman. *When Generations Collide.* New York: First Collins Business, 2005.

Luntz, Frank. *Words That Work: It's not what you say, it's what people hear.* New York: Hyperion, 2007.

Maccoby, Michael. *The Leaders We Need and What Makes Us Follow.* Boston: Harvard Business School Press, 2007.

Maltz, Maxwell. *Psychocybernetics.* New York: Pocket Books, 1969.

Martin, James. *The Meaning of the 21st Century.* London: Eden Project Books, 2006.

Miller, S.D., B.L. Duncan, & M.A. Hubble. *Escape from Babel: Toward a unifying language for psychotherapy practice.* New York: Norton, 1996.

Myers, Isabel Briggs. *Introduction to Type*, Sixth Edition. Oxford: OPP, 2000.

OPP. *Managing Stress in the Workplace.* Research report by OPP. www.opp.eu.com

Palmer, Stephen & Cary L. Cooper. *How to Deal with Stress.* London: Kogan Page, 2009.

Pollock, David C., & Ruth E. Van Reken. *Third Culture Kids: Growing Up Among Worlds.* Boston: Nicholas Brealey Publishing, 2009.

Quenk, Naomi L. *In the Grip—Understanding Type, Stress and the Inferior Function*. Palo Alto, CA: CPP Inc., 2000.

Rathus, Spencer A. *Psychology*. Orlando: Holt, Rinehart and Winston, Inc., 1990.

Rogers, Carl. *Client-Centred Therapy*. London: Constable & Robinson Ltd, 2003.

Scott, Gini Graham. *A Survival Guide for Working with Humans*. New York: AMACOM, 2004.

Sutherland, Valerie J., & Cary L. Cooper. *Strategic Stress Management: An Organisational Approach*. New York: Palgrave, 2000.

Watkins, Michael. *The First 90 Days*. USA: Harvard Business School Press, 2003.

Weil, Andrew. *Spontaneous Healing: How to Discover and Enhance Your Body's Natural Ability to Maintain and Heal Itself.* London: Warner Books, 1997.

Wilkinson, Greg. *Understanding Stress*. Dorset: Family Doctor Publications, 2004.

Williams, Stephen, & Lesley Cooper. *Managing Workplace Stress: A Best Practice Blueprint*. Chichester: John Wiley, 2002.

Wolfe, Elin L., A. Clifford Barger & Saul Benison. *Walter B. Cannon, Science and Society*. Boston: Harvard University Press, 2000.

Yapko, Michael D. *Hypnosis and the Treatment of Depression: Strategies for Change*. New York: Brunner Mazel Inc., 1992.

Yerkes, Robert M. & John Dillingham Dodson. "The Relation of Strength of Stimulus to Rapidity of Habit-Formation." *Journal of Comparative Neurology and Psychology*, 18, pp. 459–482, 1908.

Acknowledgements

To all those we have worked with in the world of work who have come on our programmes, to the people who have organized managing pressure courses, and to those at the top who have approved them and invested in the well-being of their people, a very big thank you.

Our thanks to Tina Jacobs, for her insightful and encouraging editorial comments and suggestions in preparing the manuscript.

We would also like to thank our publisher, Martin Liu, for approaching us in the first place and for his constant support. and our editor, Justin Lau, for working with us in finalizing this book.

We hope that this book will help as many people as possible. It is our firm belief that the more we are able to act transparently, authentically, compassionately and fairly, the easier it is to manage pressure and stay happy and healthy.

About the authors

Denis Sartain is a resident of New Zealand and a great fan of the country and its people. Born in Hong Kong to an English father and Chinese mother, he uses his cultural background to work with people worldwide.

From a background as a ship-broker in London, Hong Kong, Singapore and Sydney, Denis has built up the business over the past 15 years to be a favoured supplier of tailored personal-development and behavioural-change programmes for a wide range of organizations.

He is a trained in clinical hypnosis, has run training for hospital consultants and general practitioners, and is much in demand as an executive coach by senior managers. His coaching clients include Orange plc, CIPD, Anglo American, Johnson & Johnson, The Wellcome Trust, Technicolor and several top UK legal firms.

Denis is External Faculty at Henley Business School at the University of Reading, one of the world's top business schools. He also recently co-authored *Coaching Essentials: Practical, Proven Techniques for World Class Executive Coaching* (September 2009).

Maria Katsarou brings a wealth of hands-on corporate experience to the areas of coaching and executive development, having been employed with several major companies. She has worked in senior roles with leading multinationals including SCA Hygiene, Johnson & Johnson and Henkel-Ecolab (Athens and Düsseldorf), where she was responsible for providing the strategic direction, development, support, coordination and control of all HR activities.

Her last full-time role was HR director of Diageo Greece and Turkey. She has led initiatives that included setting up a Human Resources Department, embedding HR process and systems, introducing and being a catalyst for organizational change, as well as leading multi-cultural leadership programmes in Greece, Germany, South Africa, Eastern Europe and Turkey.

Maria grew up in Lagos, Nigeria, and is now based in Athens. She has a bachelor's degree in management and organizational behaviour, and master's degrees in human resources management and in psychology.

Maria is certified by the British Psychology Society to deliver MBTI, FIRO-B, CPI and 16PF, among other psychometric tools. She has tutored in management at the American College of Greece and also teaches at other academic institutions. She is a practising coach, holds the Henley Certificate in Coaching, and is on the Henley Register of Coaches. Fluent in English, French, German and Greek, Maria brings her international experience to the coaching and development environment.

Maria is co-founder of Our World Group, which specializes in running tailored in-house stress-management programmes for organizations world-wide.